7⁰⁰

Sprinkled With Ruby Dust

SPRINKLED
WITH
RUBY
DUST

H. N. Swanson

WARNER BOOKS

A Warner Communications Company

Warner Books, Inc., 666 Fifth Avenue, New York, NY 10103
W A Warner Communications Company

Printed in the United States of America
First printing: October 1989

10 9 8 7 6 5 4 3 2 1

Library of Congress Cataloging-in-Publication Data

Swanson, H. N.
    Sprinkled with ruby dust / H.N. Swanson.
        p.   cm.
    ISBN 0-446-51429-2
    I. Title.
PS3569.W269S67   1989
813'.54—dc20

                                        89-40037
                                        CIP

Book design: H. Roberts

This book of memories is dedicated to my wife, Norma, she with the pretty red hair. For a long time her favorite poem has been "Jenny Kissed Me," by Leigh Hunt. I have taken the liberty of substituting "Norma" for "Jenny." The poet—who has been dead for over a hundred years—would not object, for poets are notoriously eager to share their sentiments with us.

Norma kiss'd me when we met,
Jumping from the chair she sat in;
Time, you thief, who love to get
Sweets into your list, put that in!

Say I'm weary, say I'm sad,
Say that health and wealth have miss'd me,
Say I'm growing old, but add,
Norma kiss'd me.

Contents

CONTENTS

Introduction:
A Few Remarks
About That Man

by Elmore Leonard

"Whenever I am asked what kind of writing is the most lucrative, I have to say, ransom notes."

H.N. Swanson

Everyone in the motion-picture business and the publishing field knows him as Swanie. They say, "Sure . . . Swanie, a very dear friend of mine, known him for years." Then they smile and shake their heads with a faraway look in their eyes—or is it a faintly glazed expression?—remembering the times that they went a few negotiating rounds with him. "The toughest agent I've ever dealt with," a publisher tells me and pauses, and there is the faint smile, within it the reflection of an experience he will never forget.

In the more than thirty years that H.N. Swanson has been selling the things I write, the only less-than-friendly reference to him that I can recall was made by a New York agent who represented me during a brief period in 1969. He referred to the legendary agent from Hollywood as "that Swede counter-jumper." If the charge was not motivated entirely by sour grapes, it was at least based loosely on conflicting attitudes as to how my work should be marketed.

The East Coast agent's method was to plan his approach in the quiet, deep-cushioned confines of his club, with a martini or more, believing that there was no great urgency in offering a book manuscript; the publishers would always be there. Meanwhile, on the other coast, Swanie would be lunching with a film producer at Chasen's or the Brown Derby, intent on pitching a story, convinced that nine out of ten times the best way to sell the goods was when they were fresh out of the oven, still hot, and for as much as you could get up front. Anything else, such as profit participation in lieu of hard cash, might sound enticing but was mere pie in the sky—unless you could get points, as well as a sizable payment.

At last, after a manuscript of mine had languished in the New York agent's office for an entire month before he even knew it was there, I determined that Swanie would be my sole agent of record from that time on.

Before this—going back to the mid-fifties, when I was writing Westerns—Swanie had handled the negotiations of my first three movie deals for Marguerite Harper, who was my New York agent at the time. In August 1966, I finished my first novel with a contemporary setting; it was called *Mother, This Is Jack Ryan*. Marguerite Harper liked it, saw film possibilities in it, and immediately sent the manuscript to Swanie. (Shortly afterward, because of illness, she asked him to handle the book sale as well. Early the following year, Marguerite passed away.)

Then one morning in mid-September, the phone rang and I spoke to H.N. Swanson for the first time. He asked if I had actually written this offbeat novel about a guy named Jack Ryan—surprised, I suppose, because it wasn't a Western. I convinced him that I was the author, and Swanie's next line was one I will remember for as long as I live: "Well, kiddo, I'm going to make you rich."

I know for a fact that I believed him, because it gave my confidence a shot I can still feel today.

Even when the book drew dozens of rejections from publishers and film producers, Swanie and I knew that it would eventually sell—once I rewrote it, added a stronger plot, and changed the title to *The Big Bounce* (though I still prefer *Mother, This Is Jack Ryan*). What I didn't do, sailing now on Swanie-inspired confidence, was to take the advice of numerous editors and turn the book into a formula story.

"Don't lose your nerve now," Swanie said in a letter he wrote me in July 1967. "We have a tiger by the tail. I would suggest that you do what you're planning to do to it [the manuscript], but do it fast."

By the time I was into my next book, I felt that I should have an agent in New York as well as Swanie in Hollywood—someone to replace Marguerite Harper and deal with publishers directly. All Swanie said was, "Why? I have a phone." He didn't press the matter, and it wasn't long before I learned that Swanie's phone was more effective in the publishing marketplace than the interim agent's living presence. And that was that.

*   *   *

My first trip to Hollywood was in 1943, before going into the Navy. I hitched a ride out with a couple of high-school buddies, and we hung around Hollywood and Vine most of the time, looking for movie stars. We spotted Tyrone Power and Annabella, Helmut Dantine, Richard Whorf; visited Twentieth Century Fox and watched Betty Grable loop a number for PIN-UP GIRL; rode the Santa Monica bus past Ciro's and The Mocambo on our way to the beach—past the Swanson Building too, on Sunset Strip, but failed to notice it.

When finally I did visit Swanie's offices twenty-five years later, it was just as though I had stepped off that Santa Monica bus back in the forties. I climbed the stairs of the Swanson Building to Swanie's second-floor office of dark wood, wall sconces, venetian blinds, and a thousand books. A silver-haired gentleman in a double-breasted, pin-striped suit, a carnation in the buttonhole, said, "Well, kiddo, welcome to Hollywood." And there was no doubt in my mind but that I was there.

On that first trip, Swanie took me to the major studios in his black Cadillac and introduced me to many producers. "So they can take a look at you. They like to see what they're buying," he told me. He drove me past his three-acre, walled estate in Beverly Hills, pointing out that the way to find his home was to "look for the only house on the street without a mortgage."

A few years later (I think it was in 1973), we drove past the house again. Neighbors over the years—Dean Martin, Kenny Rogers, Pia Zadora, Linda Evans, and Frank Sinatra a couple of blocks over—come and go. Swanie, with his beautiful flower gardens and dozens of orange trees, has been there longer than any of them.

Quite unexpectedly, in January 1984, my wife Joan and I were invited to Swanie's home, to actually walk inside for the first time. On other occasions, Joan and Swanie had usually discussed investments or gardening, or argued about titles. This time they talked about movie stars who had been invited there to parties, Swanie showing us the patio where Scott and Zelda had danced. Finally I happened to mention that in the thirty years Swanie had been representing me, he had driven me past the house twice but this was the first time I had ever been inside. Swanie chuckled and said, "Well, you weren't making any real money till lately."

There was a feeling that this was a special occasion, not one to simply commemorate our first visit. In due time, Swanie announced, "I almost forgot to tell you, Norma and I got married yesterday." Swanie's first wife of fifty-two years had passed away two or three years previously. Norma had long been a friend of the family. An attractive redhead for the silver-haired lion, Norma has style and she's fun; their marriage was the best thing that could have happened to Swanie.

Still, I had to ask, "Are you telling us that you took time off from work yesterday to get married?"

Swanie growled, but with a gleam in his eye: "Of course not. Norma picked me up at four o'clock."

During the football season, the man will tolerate a weekend away from business. But anything that threatens to keep him from the office longer than that—a national holiday popping up unexpectedly, for instance—will bring forth a grumbling sound from deep within. A few years ago, following a brief illness, he wrote to say: "I'm back in the saddle and riding hard. If I never told you before, I will tell you now: nothing in this world can take the place of work. It's the best companion you will ever have. It will never upset your lifestyle, and there is always the chance it will make you rich as well as famous."

There are times when I seriously believe that he would like to see me chained to my typewriter. Once when I fractured an ankle playing tennis, his response was: "Painful though it is, I feel the accident to your leg is the best thing that has happened to your career in a long time. It means you can't be out chasing those dangerous tennis balls and will have to sit still and write all the time."

On another occasion he explained, as though I

didn't know: "The purpose of this letter is to put a burr under your saddle. I hope you are drinking large quantities of black coffee and getting that new story licked into shape."

Work, work, work.

"Hope you can finish up the job for C.F. so we can get you something else in a hurry." And there's this one: "Keep me in daily touch and stop these delightful holiday trips."

Swanie tries to motivate me whenever he sends me a check: "You should be able to live on this for two and a half years, which would free your mind of earthly cares, giving you all this time for writing."

He offers me sound financial advice. Here are just a few of his admonitions:

• Remember, the trick is to be highly solvent at all times. Preserve capital.

• Capital is a nervous rabbit ducking from under one bush to another at the slightest smell of movement anywhere. Capital is almost always in motion, so go with the flow.

• Don't follow the prices [of stocks] in the paper, because when you see a paper profit, you're likely to want to sell, and that is wrong nine times out of ten.

• If you need money, turn to your trade. You work all your life at it, and the time you give it now will raise more money for you than anything else I can think of.

• Loan no money to friends. It will get around

that you are writing for movie stars, and they will come at you from all angles.

• Protect capital! When times get rough, as they always do, loan yourself money. If you have anything left out of this check, buy your wife a pretty little hat and for yourself a pair of stylish but sturdy boots. Then back to your trade.

• The Swanson Market Letter of last week omitted a favorite of mine, Texas Oil and Gas. . . ."

*   *   *

Although Swanie has long been enamored of the movie business, he once warned me: "I know I don't have to tell you to avoid having anything to do with putting money in motion pictures or TV. They are probably the most hazardous things open to any sucker in this country at the moment."

He saw the major studios during a tight-money, low-production period as "big wet birds sitting on a telephone line trying to keep each other warm."

He continues to urge that I write stronger roles for women, adding at the bottom of a letter: "Before you go to sleep every night, I hope you review the day's writing and are pleased that the girl in the book has so much to do."

Or he may finish his letter on a note that's apropos of nothing:

• Keep all doors locked. Help is on the way.
• Take your swine-flu shot and two shots of Jack Daniels.

- We have some very good suits under $35.00 and a wide selection from which to choose.
- Whenever I am asked what kind of writing is the most lucrative, I have to say, ransom notes. (My favorite.)

In a letter to a publisher with whom he has been negotiating a contract, he adds a postscript that wonders, "Were you ever a district attorney?"

A publisher complains in outrage that Swanie is asking an unreasonable amount of money for one of my books. He won't pay it. The good-natured agent manages a resigned shrug. "Fine. If you don't want the boy, we'll go up the street." Then he adds with a grin, "We're all friends."

"The boy" witnesses another negotiating session wherein Swanie advises the publisher that the advance on a book already under contract would have to be increased by a considerable amount. The publisher protests, "But that's not fair. We have an agreement." And Swanie, with some surprise, counters with, "Fair? I never said I was fair. Do you want the boy or not?"

The fact that "the boy" is twenty years older than the publisher, and by now an old hand at the business, is beside the point. By listening to his agent, "the boy" has the feeling that he is just beginning to show what he can do.

God love him. Swanie gives you the confidence to stay with your work and to continue trying to make it better. He will tell you that it's like playing a game: though you're out to win, you don't want to take it too seriously. If it isn't fun, it isn't worth doing.

To know Swanie as a friend, and to have had him represent my work for so many years, has been one of the great pleasures of my life.

Elmore Leonard
Birmingham, Michigan
September 8, 1988

CHAPTER

1

Beginnings

Because this is a one-of-a-kind story, I'm beginning it by taking some of my own advice to the writers I represent: "First show them your credits. Let them know what you've done." That way, other people know where the writer is coming from—the roads he's taken, the choices he's made, the dreams he's pursuing. That last one is really important: the dreams he's pursuing. I guess you could say that this book is the end product of a lifetime of pursuing dreams . . . and making them come true.

I started my literary career as a magazine writer. Then I published two novels and had a play produced by Hale Flanagan. I also founded a magazine called *College Humor*—a national institution in its day—which I ran for eight years. Later, after David O.

Selznick of RKO Pictures brought me to Hollywood, I produced thirteen feature films. I also produced a weekly radio show. In the 1930s, I started my own literary agency in Hollywood . . . and I am still working at it with gusto.

Now that you have some idea of what I'm talking about, let's go back to the beginning.

* * *

I was born in a small Iowa town. No radios then. No television. But a boy could turn to books . . . and I fell head-over-heels in love with books, and with the writers who wrote them. They brought adventure, romance, and a heightened perspective on the world I did not yet know. For me, books created magic. With a rush of excitement, I realized that writers were special people. They could do no wrong. They were sprinkled with ruby dust.

Out of my small allowance I bought books at the local store, sometimes for ten cents each. Mr. Barlow, who ran the largest book and magazine store in our town, was amused at the avidity with which I purchased more . . . and more . . . and more volumes. He gave me all the magazines from which he had torn the covers in order to get credit for unsold copies. Once he gave me more than a dozen novels that had been damaged by a rain leak. Our home was bursting with the written word, until my father called a stop to it. I had adventure stories, sea stories, war stories, animal stories . . . you name it, I had it.

I guess that in high school I was a real show-off. I would correct the history teacher on facts and dates. My English teacher, tired of my heckling, suggested that I give the students tips on how to prepare their assignments for the day. Not sensing his irony, I did just that—in the face of rapidly plummeting popularity with my peers. To my credit, though, I was editor of the school paper, as well as an honor student.

In my senior year of high school, our history teacher offered a prize for an essay on any subject the class had discussed. I chose to write about my Swedish forefathers. Very little of my essay was taken from the printed page of our history lessons; most of it came from my grandfather's reminiscences. He had come to America in a sailing vessel with a score of Swedish dissenters. He was part of the colony that the group established in Bishop Hill, Illinois, where the government had given each colonist a plot of land. I put a lot of feeling and color into my essay—and it won first prize, a twenty-dollar gold coin. I ran home and presented the coin to my father, and at that moment I knew that I had stepped across the threshold of childhood and was becoming a man. I had a purpose in life now, with a goal I wanted desperately to achieve.

My father gave me a long, searching look. "Son," he said, "I guess I never knew until now how much you wanted to be a writer." Then the tears came. I had never before seen him cry, and it made me feel like crying too. He said, "You better be a good one!"

Around this time I realized that I would have

to make my own way in life, because my parents had a very meager income. Therefore I pursued every avenue within my reach to earn money. I took a job working at the local county fairs as a shill for ex-Army pilots who had their own Jennies from World War I. I would sit in the cockpit encouraging people to take a ride in one of these flying machines. The pilots thought that working the farm belt was pretty tame stuff after having been under fire during the War. They would take the farmers up for a dollar a minute, giving them scary rides with their fancy flying tricks such as dead-stick dives, rolls, and loop-the-loops. I myself was scared stiff . . . but the pay was good.

I took a course in Gregg shorthand, which got me a job as a court reporter for a few months. I talked my way into a job with the Burlington Railroad in Centerville, Iowa. My duties consisted of keeping daily track of where the company's freight cars were on other lines. A freight car often traveled several times across the country before it came home, and during that time, it earned a daily fee for the company that owned it.

2

A Higher Education

Soon after this, I received a scholarship to Grinnell College in Grinnell, Iowa. There I found my studies easy enough, but the struggle to survive was tough. Although my folks sent me some money from time to time, essentially I was on my own. I worked in the college business office doing clerical chores, for which I received a whopping twenty-five cents an hour.

To raise spending money was the real problem. I tried to economize on food. For dessert I would order either a piece of pie or a dish of ice cream, but never pie a-la-mode. Because my laundry bill was a burden, I sent my laundry home to my mother, who would wash and iron it . . . and send it back with a batch of homemade fudge.

Occasionally one of the students who knew that

I had a typewriter would hire me to prepare a theme paper. In this way I became a writer for hire ... except when my employer would simply forget to pay me. I even started a laundry concession in the men's dormitory. And I had a raccoon coat that I had bought in Chicago during a sale at Marshall Field's. This coat not only took a lot of punishment from me, but eventually I rented it out to a couple of guys for wearing on weekends, including while at football games. This venture lasted for quite a while ... until the fur fell out in clumps and it looked like a plucked chicken.

It might have been this tight financial situation that further launched me on a career as a writer. I began to write for magazines. I churned out impossibly true stories for *True Confessions*, sold epigrams to *The Smart Set*, and even broke into the "how-to" field by inventing a new way to hang pictures.

I sold stories to *Judge* and to the old *Life* magazine, and timely checks from both helped out. The fattest checks, however, came from my steamy love stories for the pulps. I found a New York literary agent, Robert Thomas Hardy. His first sale on my behalf was to a lively magazine with the marvelous name of *Saucy Stories*. The year was 1922, and I earned the sum of $13.50 for my story; Hardy wrote to me, trying to soften the fiscal blow by shaving his commission. The date was August 22, a day that will live in infamy. Hardy's letter is still proudly framed in my office, where clients look at it in wonder.

*   *   *

Grinnell had less than eight hundred students in those days, and half of them were men. Everyone knew everyone else. One of my friends was a long string bean of a fellow from Montana named Gary Cooper. The college kids called him "Cowboy Cooper" with their inevitable sarcasm. One day a senior brought a sleepy milk-wagon horse on campus. He walked up to the Montana cowboy and said, "Coop, here's a really fiery steed. Can you ride it?" Without hesitation, Coop jumped on, dug his heels into the horse's belly, and took off in a cloud of dust. There was no more kidding after that. From that day on, "Cowboy Cooper" was a big fella on campus.

On my trips to California I would often stay at Cooper's house. He had a big flame-out with Lupe Velez. They would fight like hell. Like two cats. Then they would sit down, have drinks, and eat great quantities of tacos. Cooper, who generally looked like a sleepy kind of a guy, as though the blood didn't circulate too well, would flush with excitement when he had it out with Lupe. Well, I've heard it said that some people thrive on arguments. But Coop was always a kind man, and a good friend to me. He was such a strong man, so wonderfully put together, that I knew he would never die.

*   *   *

F. Scott Fitzgerald's *This Side of Paradise* was sweeping the country at this time. Scott was the kind of writer who *really* had ruby dust. I was determined to meet him, somewhere, sometime. A few years later, when it happened that we became friends, I showed him my copy of *This Side of Paradise*. All of the purple passages were carefully marked, and in the margins there were extensive and enthusiastic comments on style. Scott was moved by the condition of the book, realizing that it was symbolic of how many college students had enjoyed it.

"Is it too poetic?" he asked me.

"Hell, no!" I answered.

Then we talked at length about college sex. I was now in a place where morals were free and easy, or so I thought. At least the girls in my hometown had never rolled their stockings! I was a virgin, and all of this confused me.

At the same time, I was involved in projects that paid me little but were very satisfying. The college newspaper sought some of my time, and I became editor of the college humor magazine, *The Malteaser*. I tried out for the drama club and was instructed to read the line, "I love you," three times. I delivered it with such intensity that I was greeted by gales of laughter. I got into the club.

A book of my verses came out during my senior year. I took to the road in my old trusty-rusty Ford during the summer vacation and sold the book throughout Iowa, Illinois, Missouri, Nebraska, and Kansas. I discovered that selling was much easier than writing, leading me to decide that I would rather be a mover and a shaker than a writer.

CHAPTER

3

I Start Out

I left Grinnell with a dummy of a national magazine, to be called *The College Widow*. I wanted it to be a bright, sophisticated, and youthful production, with short stories illustrated by name artists, loaded with cartoons, and carrying the best from the current college-humor magazines. I was partly influenced by *The Smart Set*, run by H.L. Mencken and George Jean Nathan.

I had no money, of course, so I felt that I must locate either in Chicago or New York in order to find a backer. My uncle, John Norling, put me up in his large house on the North Side of Chicago. He had once been the publisher of the *Svenska Tribune*, one of the largest foreign-language newspapers in the country.

Uncle John looked over my prospectus and put me in touch with John Lansinger, formerly the successful head of subscription sales for *Pictorial Review*. Lansinger, a graduate of Franklin and Marshall, was a really nice guy. We talked for a couple of days and then he said that he would put up the money "to try out what you've got," but added that the magazine would have to be called *College Humor*.

As editor, I spread my skimpy editorial budget to its limit while pursuing every friendly face. At the age of twenty-three, I was the youngest editor of any national magazine in the country. I was just a kid from the corn belt, with a head full of crazy dreams and a magazine that had not yet come off the presses—but it sure as hell would.

Anyway, I was now in business. Whether or not the magazine would succeed was a roll of the dice. Our office was a walk-up. It consisted of two rooms on Chestnut off La Salle. Working conditions were not ideal. John Lansinger and I faced each other across a big desk. Since we were reprinting the best material we could find in humor magazines from approximately thirty colleges, our callers were mostly young college editors who came to see what we were doing. We were there every day, including Sundays and holidays.

But as hard as we worked, we played just as hard. We had great meals at the Drake and Ambassador hotels because we had due bills whereby we traded advertising space in the magazine for food. It was truly a gourmet caper, with flaming swordsteaks and red liquor. We ate there like pigs and had a wonderful time.

Part of my job as a magazine editor was to cover as many football games during the season as possible. I think my bones are still cold from sitting so long and so often in the rain and snow, because in those days there were no stadiums. If you wanted to see Red Grange tear down the field like nobody before, you had to undergo some hardships.

But it was fun. On weekdays, Lansinger and I often found ourselves playing host to young editors from schools around Chicago. They would drop by without warning and expect us to buy them dinner and show them the nightclubs. Since Prohibition was in full swing, "Joe College" did what his peers were doing all across the land: he got anesthetized on near beer laced with ether; he saturated himself with the best Al Capone Scotch; in general, he got stoned on anything that would give him a big bump in a hurry. Usually we took these visitors down to Colisimo's on 22nd Street on the South Side.

While the band was playing "Whispering" and the hoods were bumping around with their big mammas, our guests managed to get themselves pretty dizzy. They would finally reach a point where they would need a little air, and we would deposit them outside in their cars, first taking their watches and money so that the parking-lot boys wouldn't clean them out. After a while, they would reappear, full of charm and vigor, ready to move in on the gangsters' girls.

4

Casting
the Net

My first experience in
buying material from a writer was with H.C. Witwer.
He had been having success with his humorous
books and had made a trip to Chicago to present his
latest story. I lunched, dined, and stayed up forever,
listening to his ideas until he passed out. He asked
a very big price for his story. I offered him one tenth
of the amount, which he accepted instantly. He then
tore out the washbowl in his room by the roots. The
Edgewater Beach Hotel regretfully ejected him. I began to think about casting my net more widely.

I went to New York and checked in at the Algonquin Hotel, which hosted the kind of writers I
wanted to attract. Robert Benchley was my first contact, and he outlined an article that I bought on the
spot. Then I went across the street to the Royalton,

which housed George Jean Nathan, Mencken's partner in *The Smart Set*. Nathan had a rococo apartment crowded with theatrical memorabilia and photographs of the stars. I think he was amused to learn that I was a former contributor to his magazine, the source of those cynical epigrams about love and marriage, though only a kid. He became one of my biggest boosters.

Usually Mencken would come up from Baltimore every two weeks to stay at the Algonquin, arriving with a little old-fashioned valise that contained only a nightshirt and two bottles of Scotch. I nailed him fast. He said, "I know all about Grinnell. One of my best writers, Ruth Suckow, came from there." He had praise for a young writer he had discovered, Sara Haardt, who wrote a brand of humorous dialogue then fashionable at schools everywhere. She became one of my regular contributors, and to the surprise of no one, later became Mrs. Mencken.

*   *   *

I had been watching Scott Fitzgerald's work for so long that it reached the point where I simply had to meet him. I contacted his literary agent, Harold Ober, and asked him if he could arrange an appointment. I said that since my magazine appealed to the younger crowd, it was almost imperative that I get something by Scott in our publication—not just once, but regularly.

Ober set up an appointment to meet at his office on Manhattan's 49th Street. I got there before Scott. When he arrived, he was in a depressed state, but looking handsome in college-cut clothes. After we shook hands, he said with a soft smile, "I think I need a drink. How about you?"

Two hours later we knew one another pretty well. I was surprised to learn that he was a steady reader of *College Humor*. Scott especially liked the series we were running about famous colleges and universities; every month a well-known writer jumped at the chance to sentimentalize about his alma mater. Scott agreed to do a piece about Princeton, and our relationship had begun.

Later, when I met a white-faced and corpulent Alexander Woollcott, I told him about our series of articles on famous colleges by their eminent alumni. Woollcott said immediately, "I'll write about my school, Hamilton."

The college series proved a success. Some of the contributors included J.P. McEvoy, who wrote about Notre Dame; Gene Markey on Dartmouth; Lois Long, who wrote on Vassar; Ruth Suckow on Grinnell; Gilbert Seldes on Harvard; Bernard De Voto on Northwestern; and there were dozens of others. For the first time, I felt that the whole country was looking at my magazine.

*   *   *

Soon I came to realize that I was making a mistake in negotiating directly with the writers themselves. Any writer who was worth anything had an agent. My next move, therefore, was to meet about two dozen New York literary agents and sell them the idea that we were going to do something new:

put out a magazine of youth by youth. I found these agents to be very receptive, and friendships developed between us that were satisfying and useful later on. They understood that my editorial budget was tight and tried to go along with me.

I knew that I would have to line up several top illustrators to enhance the fiction that I was beginning to buy. I contacted James Montgomery Flagg and Arthur William Brown for the four-part serials that had started to run. I also recruited Garrett Price, Ralph Barton, and Russell Patterson. I soon made a contract with Rolph Armstrong to put a girl on the cover every month, and what beautiful girls they were. Once Rudy Vallee called me to ask for the phone number of one of these striking young women. I gave it to him . . . and one month later they were married.

I put the work of John Held, Jr., on the cover once, and thereafter his wonderful black-and-whites were all over every issue. He embellished a series by Groucho Marx with some wonderful woodcuts. John Held, Jr., along with F. Scott Fitzgerald, truly captured the spirit of the flapper and the Jazz Age.

* * *

I wanted the magazine to have real "class." I wanted a writer for every issue whose work was being talked about and who would sell to young people. It seemed to me that Noel Coward was perfect for this. I cornered him backstage in his dressing room in New York after a performance one night. He was then a young man, with great energy shining from his eyes. Coward had a terrific asset: he gave enormous concentration to the person with whom he was talking.

He amazed me when he said that he had been interested by several pieces in various issues of the magazine. Above all, he loved the jokes. Coward told me that all of the show-business comedians, "and some who aren't," relied on *College Humor* for material to use in their acts. I responded by telling him how much I admired his *Private Lives*. He gave me a long look. "Did it really work for you?" he asked. "I'm curious, because I wanted to grab the youngest audience I could, not just the older folks." I told him that it was perfectly suited to appeal to our readership.

"My friend," he said, "if you mean that, I would like to see it appear in a jolly magazine like yours."

I told Coward that I was flattered but that my editorial budget was too small to pay his going rate. "You owe me nothing for it," he said. "Let's hope it lifts your heart a little."

Not only would Coward not take a cent for it, but he also included his wonderful song, "Someday I'll Find You." The last thing he said to me was, "Swanie, you're young. You may have magic, but you probably don't realize it. Stay young—nothing can stop you."

Noel Coward lived in Manhattan's strange and wonderful Hotel Des Artistes at 1 West 67th Street, which had also been home to dancer Isadora Duncan, heartthrob Rudolph Valentino, and many others. The manager of the Hotel Des Artistes was a well-known spiritualist and medium who held seances on the premises. Another famous resident, Harry Houdini, was also known to produce visitors from the spirit world from time to time. Once I asked Harry how he did it and he told me that the secret of the trick resided with the lady who was his assistant and who concealed a length of cheesecloth in a certain part of her anatomy.

"It's luminescent, you know," the great Houdini assured me, referring to the cheesecloth.

C H A P T E R

5

Scott

Harold Ober arranged several meetings for me with F. Scott Fitzgerald, which resulted in our making an arrangement for Scott and his wife, Zelda, to do a series of vignettes about the girls of the day. One time Scott said to me, "Zelda thinks she can write; I've read some of her sketches and I feel that they are exceptionally good. Would you read one of them and encourage her to keep at it?"

I quickly agreed, and that day I received a copy of Zelda's "Southern Girl." I thought it brilliant in spite of its disorganization. I bought it, and after that I ran her "Follies Girl" and three or four of her other short stories in *College Humor*. Here is the foreword I wrote for the copy on "Southern Girl":

You know how sweethearts have a song between them, one they have grown to like very much. When they are separated and this song is played, their song, for them it immediately recalls the happiness they shared, and those dusty words, "I love you."

Examine carefully "Southern Girl," which the Fitzgeralds have done for this issue. There is not one line of conversation in it, but with very few words, they have struck out a soft pattern of beauty, and characters who were so real in their own lives that they come alive in your own. I am so happy to have it because it marks an important milestone in the literary career of Zelda Fitzgerald. I cannot imagine any girl having a richer background than Zelda's, a life more crowded with interesting people and events.

Scott asked me to read a novel he had just completed, called *Trimalchio of West Egg*. I thought it the best thing of his that I had ever read, but I told him, "That's a horrible title!"

"Really?" he asked. "Why don't you like it?"

"I think it would kill any book sale," I answered.

"I guess you're right, as so many other people have told me the same thing."

I suggested that he call it "Gatsby," or "The Great Gatsby." To this he replied, "I'll have to make my final decision when I finish it, which will be very soon."

But of course it wasn't very soon. Scott had to do a little more living first. He and Zelda were the golden kids of the Jazz Age. They had invented it, and their exploits showed the world how to live it. That included jumping into the fountain at the Plaza, going overboard on a sailing date, and partying from dusk until dawn.

Scott and Zelda might have been the Crazy Kids of the Twenties, but one thing to be said for them is that they were very good parents to Scottie, a darling little girl as bright as one of the brass buttons on her brand-new coat. If she was sometimes bewildered by the speed at which the world was spinning around her, she kept her balance somehow. She was a beautiful child, and her parents always conversed with her in French.

Zelda was almost obsessed with ballet. Scott told me, "She's too old now to make a name for herself as a ballet dancer, and her figure would not sustain it." She regularly took ballet lessons, insisting on paying for them personally from her magazine sales. Of course her daughter, Scottie, had to take lessons too.

Scott's strange and cavalier attitude toward money was well known. He may have developed it early in life; at the age of ten, he wrote to his mother from Camp Chatham:

> Please send me a dollar because there are a lot of little odds and ends I need. I will spend it cautiously. All the other boys have pocket money besides their regular allowance.

Scott's father, Edward, may have helped the youthful Scott to develop his unique style as far as money was concerned. Here is a letter to his twelve-year-old son:

I enclose $1.00. Spend it liberally, generously, carefully, judiciously, sensibly. Get from it pleasure, wisdom, health, and experience.

When I read *The Great Gatsby*, I made an offer to Harold Ober of $25,000 for the first serial rights. Scott was delighted, but Scribners talked him out of it, feeling that it might adversely affect the sale of the book. I told Scott that it was probably the worst thing that had happened to me to date. Of course the book went on to become a memorable hit, and it seems to be the one work of his most likely to live forever.

Scott was a good critic of his own work. I remember a section in *Gatsby* that described a very emotional scene with Zelda. It ran for over four pages in length, and the writing was terrific, but Scott crossed it all out and wound up with only four words: "They fell in love." For a long time, the original manuscript of *The Great Gatsby* was in my office files. Unfortunately, some light-fingered individual knew this and stole it.

*   *   *

Throughout most of his later life, Scott was hard-pressed for money. His health was flagging, and Zelda's medical bills, incurred as she went in and out of mental hospitals, took a great toll on their finances. When the big magazines stopped paying him the large prices he had formerly commanded, he turned to writing plays. These, like "The Vegetable," were unsuccessful. Book royalties dwindled. He started a series of stories about Pat Hobby for *Esquire*, but the income was small even though they bought as much material as he could give them.

Sadly, Scott blamed some of his money problems on Harold Ober, who always came to his rescue. Scott would ignore the problem until a crisis developed. When his debit balance became uncomfortably high, Ober would call to ask me to get Scott a picture deal, which I did, and it allowed him to shore up his cash position for a while.

Hollywood gave Scott opportunities to write for the screen many times, but nothing really came of it. The main reason for this was that he never quite understood the medium. He thought that one writer could create two hours of entertainment with very little help from other artists.

Scott was a writer of novels, which was the only kind of writing to arouse his creative being. He felt that the producers to whom he was usually assigned had low emotional levels, little understanding of life, and poor taste. Time and time again he was handed what the studios believed was a prize property. If he accepted an assignment, he usually failed to sustain his interest and he would have to be taken off the schedule. Then he would become highly vocal about the fact that he must be on a "studio black list." Scott was out of place living and working in Hollywood.

It is thanks to Fitzgerald's daughter, Scottie, that Princeton Library is the custodian of her father's material. His letters convey a fine and sensitive literary mind, as well as a reflection of the relationships that so dramatically influenced his life and work.

* * *

Ernest Hemingway said that Scott was a "cry baby" and that he himself had very little respect for cry babies. Nevertheless, many letters passed between Scott and Ernest that reveal their regard for one another. One such letter from Scott reads:

> Dear Ernest, It's a fine novel. Better than anybody else writing could do. Thanks for thinking of me and for your dedication. I read it with intense interest, participating in a lot of the writing problems as they came along and often quite unable to discover how you brought off some of the effects, but you always did. The massacre was magnificent and also the fight on the mountain and the actual dynamiting scene.

And in another letter from Fitzgerald to Hemingway:

> I think it is obvious that my respect for your artistic life is absolutely unqualified, that save for a few of the dead or dying old men, you are the only man writing fiction in America that I look up to very much.

But later, when Hemingway mentioned Scott in *The Snows of Kilimanjaro*, Scott wrote:

Dear Ernest, Please lay off me in print. If I choose to write *de profundis* sometimes, it doesn't mean I want friends praying aloud over my corpse. No doubt you meant it kindly, but it cost me a night's sleep. And when you incorporate it (the story) in a book, would you mind cutting my name. It's a fine story, one of your best—even though the "poor Scott Fitzgerald," etc., rather spoiled it for me.

After Hemingway's nonfiction book, *A Moveable Feast*, was published, and after I had moved on to Hollywood, Hemingway asked me to try to sell it as a motion picture. I told him that while it would undoubtedly please his readership, it would probably be difficult to sell it to film producers.

CHAPTER

6

Chicago, Chicago

Meanwhile, our magazine prospered. We moved into a three-story office building that had been built for the American Telephone & Telegraph Company. And I meant built; it was all steel and concrete. I knew that if a bomb were ever dropped on Chicago, the building would still be standing. It was on La Salle in Chicago's North Side. Our editorial department took over the entire third floor. People in the building knew we were up there because there was always a lot of hootin' and hollerin' going on.

While circulation showed gratifying growth, we still had to spend money carefully. We needed to serialize some book-length features but couldn't quite afford the high fees involved. I solved this problem by writing a couple of novels myself: *Big Busi-*

ness Girl and *They Fell in Love*. The first of these I wrote with my associate editor, Patricia Reilly. After we serialized it, it was published by Farrar-Strauss and promptly bought for films as a starring vehicle for Loretta Young. We also serialized my second book, which was later published by Harcourt Brace.

My editorial specialty was the discovery of new writers. No issue ever went to press without at least one story that was a first for the writer. I found Katherine Brush from East Liverpool, Ohio, and her output became a quick success. Her first novel, *Glitter*, was a hit with the fans, and her *Little Sins* really lit up the night sky. I had been dealing directly with her because she had no agent, but I convinced her that now she was in the big time and should be appearing in *The Saturday Evening Post*.

Harold Ober became Katherine's agent, and she remained with him for the rest of her life. Kay's novels were quickly bought and exploited by the *Post*. Her *Young Men of Manhattan* and *Redheaded Woman* were also successful movies. She moved to New York and had an apartment with a living room two stories high, decorated by Joseph Urban. She was living it up.

*   *   *

One day a white-faced, bizarre-looking creature in a black overcoat reaching to his toes came to see me. He said that his name was Cornell Woolrich, and he stressed the fact that he was a good writer. He then pushed a script at me and fled. It was an excellent story, and I was the first editor with whom he had had any success. We published this story and many more of his.

Woolrich wrote a novel, *Children of the Ritz*, that won our "Campus Novel Contest." I made two trips to California within seven weeks to try to pass along some of my enthusiasm for it to film producers. I engendered enough interest that a movie deal appeared before the book was published. Woolrich was only twenty-one years old at the time and had infinite promise. In later years, he sold most of his output to Alfred Hitchcock.

*   *   *

Most of the years I spent in Chicago were golden years. My business interests had expanded to include more than just *College Humor*. A number of publishers had seen how successful our first magazine was and wanted to get in on a good thing. As a technique of mystifying the opposition, we launched a few similar magazines. In effect, we became our own competition! This kept me busy traveling around the country promoting our magazines in such places as New York, San Francisco, Miami Beach, Palm Beach, and even East Hampton. However, life was not *all* sweetness and light. The struggle against our competitors was a sharp one. To keep them guessing, we put out no less than three magazines with titles similar to ours.

*   *   *

Fortunately, Al Capone did not decide that we represented competition for him, or even a sweet deal that he could muscle in on. We were approached once, however, by a big, ugly man in a dark suit who was curious to know if we could use any "enforcers" in the circulation department. He was coming from Al Capone's business office in the Lexington Hotel, where Capone also lived. We thanked the man very politely for his concern and forgot the matter.

In Chicago in those days, the whine of squad cars could be heard every night, announcing that the crime pot was still boiling. If you happened to step out at night to buy a newspaper, you just might get stopped by a plainclothesman and asked for identification, then be advised to stay off the streets at night because they were so dangerous.

Such was the reign of Al Capone in Chicago. Capone was a mean-looking guy with a big, sloppy stomach and X-ray eyes; he looked as if he had crawled out of the woodwork. His hydra-headed organization involved the obvious activities of gambling, rum-running, prostitution, and drug-dealing. Less obvious was the fact that he also made strenuous efforts to hog-tie the blossoming movie industry. He almost got away with it.

In his attempt to take over the studios, Capone founded a trade union that still survives today. To extend his tentacles into the movie industry, he created a workers' union that he called the International Alliance of Theatrical and Stage Employees. Today IATSE is a powerful voice in the working lives of technicians in the movie industry and the legitimate theater.

Capone started out quietly enough as business

manager for motion-picture projectionists. Before long, he was calling all the shots. He decided the amount of dues that were to be paid as well as how much of the pension funds he could grab. When the studio workers realized what was going on and fore-saw real (as opposed to movie) violence in Holly-wood, it was too late for them to avert it. Soon murder and mayhem occurred. Apparently Holly-wood was no longer a town for kids. Capone or-chestrated his plan to capture the studios to the point that he was able to force each major studio to kick in $50,000 a year.

The Capone tentacles not only reached out to Hollywood; they also closed in on the star perform-ers of the vaudeville stage and legitimate theater. When actors played Chicago, Capone's "enforcers" would go backstage and approach them with their "protection advice." Stars such as Eddie Cantor were obliged to pay many thousands of dollars. When nightclub performer Joe E. Lewis attempted to open his own club, The Reinzi, at Clark and Diversy in Chicago, Capone—who had once hired Lewis in his own clubs—was not pleased. Joe's throat was cut, but by a miracle, his life and voice were saved.

The era of menace and violence continued until Westbrook Pegler, a fearless Chicago newspaperman, started to write regular articles exposing organized crime. "Peg" was a frequent contributor to *College Humor*. He was a close friend of Katherine Brush, and the three of us spent many times together in Miami Beach and New York.

It was common in those days to go into a restaurant and find all of the better tables taken by the mob. The mob also bought the best seats of the shows then playing in Chicago. I recall going to see "Topsy and Eva," starring the Duncan sisters, at the Woods Theater. The mob scene was almost as much fun to watch as the show. Al Capone was in attendance, with four bodyguards seated in the row ahead of him and four in the row behind. No one elbowed them aside.

We printed an article in a magazine we controlled called *Amazing Stories*. The article suggested that Capone's face was not really his own, but that he had been given a cosmetic job under orders from the New York mob. Since our Collegiate World Publishing Company listed me as editorial director of *Amazing Stories* as well as *College Humor*, the Chicago mob was able to look up my name and deduce that I had been responsible for the article. For about ten days when I left work at eight in the evening, my car was followed . . . just to let me know that they were watching.

Our office on North La Salle was in the middle of Chicago's North Side crime. One noon, as I walked back from lunch, I saw the leader of the Irish mob, Dion O'Bannion, lying dead among the roses in the window of his florist shop. O'Bannion's florist business was an attractive sideline to his other activities, since the numerous gangster funerals gave him a large and steady income. A few blocks up the street from our office there was a cathedral with a cornerstone pockmarked by the gangsters' machine guns. One of our clients, W.R. Burnett, was inspired by this to write a strong ending for his picture, HIGH SIERRA, which starred Humphrey Bogart.

*   *   *

Al Capone was not the only big operator in Chicago. There were others that you would have actually enjoyed meeting. I met William Randolph Hearst one gloomy Chicago afternoon outside the Congress Hotel on Michigan Avenue. My art director, George Eggleston, was a friend of the Hearst boys; they had spent the afternoon together in the Hearst suite making telephone calls to Paris, Rio de Janeiro, and almost anywhere else in the world that caught their imagination . . . all in fun.

When Hearst stepped out of a taxicab into a light rain that was falling, he seemed to be fumbling in his pockets for money with which to pay the cabby. I said to Eggleston, "I think I'll do my good deed for the day." Thereupon I walked over to Hearst and introduced myself by saying, "Could I help you out?" Then I slipped him a bill. I told him that I was a magazine editor and that he had always been a hero to me. He was a tall, intense man with perpetual snow on his head. He smiled, nodded, and thanked me, saying, "We'll take care of this." He never did.

Two months later, I received a New York phone call from my friend, Ray Long, editor of Hearst's *Cosmopolitan* magazine. He told me that he was retiring and that he planned to live in California. Hearst had asked him to recommend someone to take his place. "I thought of you immediately," Ray said. "Let me mention your name to Mr. Hearst."

I told Long that I was not interested in leaving Chicago, that I made as much money as I wanted, and that I had a half-interest in the magazine that I had started. Ray knew all of this, of course, and said, "I won't tell Hearst you're not interested in *Cosmopolitan*. I'm sure he wouldn't like to hear that."

About a month later, Ray called again and said, "On your next trip to Manhattan, I think you ought to meet Hearst just for the hell of it and see what happens." Ray and I agreed to meet at Ray's Manhattan club. He brought along the two Hearst boys who, incidentally, were regular readers of *College Humor*. We had a jolly lunch and then Ray said, "The old man wants me to make you an offer to rebuild *Cosmopolitan*." He mentioned a figure that was fair but not attractive enough to sway me.

"Tell him I'm making more than that each month," I said, "and that I'm my own boss." Shortly afterward, Hearst called Ray in, gave him a gold watch, a month's salary, and his blessing. That was the end of Ray's editing career. Hearst was probably lucky that I didn't take the job. Later, Helen Gurley Brown made a unique and successful publication of *Cosmo*.

* * *

The years I spent in running *College Humor* were without doubt the happiest of my life. It was really a time of wine and roses. Success came quickly, and so easily that it left enough time to enjoy life. I lived at Chicago's Ambassador West on the top floor, where they put the noisiest people. It was where the action was. The Duncan sisters had a suite, with piano music and laughter going on day and night.

Richard Bennett, the actor and father of Constance and Joan Bennett, had a kennel of prize pups in his room. He would put them in a basket and lower them by rope to the street, where waiting bellhops would take them for a walk and then give them a nice ride back upstairs. The top floor of the hotel was mainly for people who were doing shows in town. A certain amount of colorful show-business squabbling went on, but that came with the territory.

During this time, I was a bachelor. I chased all the girls, and some of them chased me. I had a long Stutz roadster, and when I put on my raccoon coat and derby hat on some of those sub-zero Chicago days, Katherine Brush said it seemed that I was reclining in a bathtub.

The Jazz Age hit the country like a streak of lightning. It was complicated by Prohibition. The stock market went through the roof, and then the roof fell in. The era was one of free and easy feeling. It brought about a change in clothing styles. Men wore bell-bottom trousers, and coats made from the skins of animals—preferably raccoons. Women's skirts were above the knee. Women rolled their stockings and bobbed their hair. Our magazine mirrored what the young people were feeling and thinking.

Started on a shoestring, *College Humor* quickly elbowed similar magazines aside and became a cult. In the eight years that I was the editorial director, we had the largest national newsstand circulation of any thirty-five-cent magazine. A great part of the success was due to the publisher, who told us that if we could avoid dependence on subscriptions, which always costs a company money, we would make it big at the newsstands. Newsstand sales gave us an accurate index of how we were doing.

Ours was an experiment that worked. It was a time when everyone felt that the only way to start out in life was to go to college. That, of course, led to Jordan roadsters and girls with wind in their hair. Young people's tastes were changing so fast that in our business, we had to try to anticipate them. We were running as fast as we could.

C H A P T E R

7

Hunting
the Quarry

People have often asked me how it is that I seem to have found so many of our well-known writers. The answer is that I met many of them before they were well known. When I glance through a magazine, it is always the stories by unknowns that I read first. A book by a new name always crooks a finger and beckons to me. An efficient-looking manuscript from a beginner is always a new adventure.

However, that did not prevent me from getting that eyes-glazed-over look when I had my sights set on a big-name writer. I guess I wrote steam-up notes to at least one hundred people whose work I admired. One of these people was Michael Arlen, author of *The Green Hat*. This was the national best-seller that prompted Donald Ogden Stewart to quip, "Not brilliant, but brilliantine." Arlen returned my note, advising that he would do a piece for me. He ended his witty letter by saying, "There is only one way to tell a story. Quickly smite the reader to the floor and then pour your story lightly over him."

I hunted my artistic quarry with complete absorption. Sometimes I trapped my game at his home, and on other occasions, at his favorite watering hole. Donald Stewart, Dorothy Parker, and Bob Benchley usually met at Manhattan saloons. Don had a cocker spaniel he brought along, and he always ordered a bowl of beer for it. I signed Benchley, who promised me two books and a play, which I proudly ran.

I went to Providence, Rhode Island, to see S.J. Perelman, whose cartoons in *The Brown Jug* brought him to our attention. He wrote the captions for the series of woodcuts illustrating the Groucho Marx pieces we ran. I tried to tell him that although his artwork was original and very funny, he was a better writer than cartoonist. I asked him to write a few paragraphs on the future for us. He went on to do a couple of books, such as *Dawn Ginsburg's Revenge*, and we printed great portions of them eventually. His days as a cartoonist were over.

MacKinlay Kantor was one of my best friends. He will be remembered for his first novel, *Diversy*, and for *The Best Years of Our Lives*. I introduced him to Sam Goldwyn, who bought *Best Years* and made a fine film from it. Goldwyn, who always had trouble with names, continued to call him "Mr. MacKinlay," and took credit for having discovered him. When BEST YEARS won an Academy Award, Sam said, "I don't care of this picture doesn't make a nickel—so long as every man, woman, and child in America sees it!"

Carl Sandburg asked me to come down to Michigan City and have a beer with him. He lived among the sand dunes and played the bongo drums when the mood was with him. Together, we ate an ungodly amount of goat cheese. He said that if he wrote a "little sliver of something," I could use it in my magazine. He did and I did.

Other stars who were caught in the Swanson net and entrapped by the magazine were Lynn and Lois Montross, who created the character of "Andy Prothero," the perennial campus lover. Adela Rogers St. Johns often wrote for *College Humor*, and when she later married Stanford football star Dick Hyland, they collaborated on a serial that we ran.

On one of my trips to Hollywood, I made friends with Walt Disney. I went out to the studio to lunch in the commissary, which was situated on "Dopey Lane." The waitress who took our order always called him "Walt." There was a wonderful spirit on the lot. Walt liked me and the magazine. To prove it, he did a double-page spread on Mickey Mouse for every issue for over a year . . . and refused to take a cent for it.

8

Hollywood

All this time my friend, David O. Selznick, head of RKO studios, had been after me to come out to Hollywood to make a "college picture." At last I succumbed because the money was good and I thought his star was rising fast. The three years that I spent at RKO were undoubtedly the roughest of my life. I had come from the magazine business, which I understood and where work was really play. Now I was in the film business, which I did not understand and where work was difficult. It was work laced with stress and anxiety. Apparently everybody in the field understood this and simply lived with it.

In the magazine business, writers were the main concern: how to find them and how to get their best work. In Hollywood, I quickly discovered that in the movie business, the important people were the star, the director, the producer . . . and, of course, the source of the production money. The writer was far down on the list, perhaps under "Miscellaneous."

I knew only a couple of stars, no directors or producers whatsoever, and no screenwriters. When I started in the business, screenwriters formed a tight little group of twenty-five to thirty-five men and women. They were generally under contract to the studios, and contrary to popular idea, they were paid very well. Of course when I began, I didn't know where the industry had come from or where it was headed. I knew no one on a studio lot employing several hundred people. I knew only David O. Selznick, and our relationship was a wonderful one, but as I accumulated time in the industry, I began to see that David was the sole reason I wanted to remain with RKO.

Selznick knew every detail that went into a motion picture. Was the photography bad because of too much backlight on an actor's hair? He attacked the smallest problem as if it were earth-shaking. His pictures were his life.

His fierce attack on the Hollywood system was partially in revenge for the manner in which the studios had treated his father, Louis J. Selznick. David thought that the big-studio moguls had conspired to squeeze this pioneer of film out of production. He never forgot this and fought hard to be his own man in Hollywood, beholden to none.

I had access to Selznick at almost any time, but

I was careful not to contact him unless I had a story that I wanted to interest him in or news that would catch his attention. As an example, I read early proofs of *State Fair*, a novel by Phil Stong. I kept telling David that it would be bought quickly by some studio and that it might even be a best-seller.

He laughed me off. "What is a state fair?" he asked. "You mean that an audience could be interested in farmers who go to a fair to exhibit prize pigs?" I finally got him to read the book, such was my enthusiasm. No luck. "Impossible property," he declared.

I wrote Selznick a daily memo for a number of weeks, telling him about the book's rise in sales. Adela Rogers St. Johns, who was on the lot as a writer, had also read the book and liked it. When she learned that I was touting it to everybody, she came to my office and said, "Kid, I assumed that you were not Phil Stong, but I must say, you are as right as hell about this book." Even though she tried, she could do nothing with Selznick.

Then, quite suddenly, Fox Studios bought *State Fair*, made a beautiful picture out of it, and remade the picture twice during subsequent years. Equally suddenly, David was impressed to the point of asking me continually, "What's hot today?" Instead of my chasing him, I found that thereafter he eagerly solicited my ideas on books, old and new.

Selznick had a strong preference for the classics. He often talked about *David Copperfield*, by Charles Dickens, and later made the picture after he went to

Metro. Once he told me that his lifelong ambition was to be a book publisher, like Bennett Cerf.

David hired F. Scott Fitzgerald to write love scenes for GONE WITH THE WIND. He had followed Scott's career from the beginning, and he bought the film rights to *Tender Is the Night* through me. He tried several dramatizations of the novel, but neither he nor Scott felt that its potential had been realized. It remained on David's list of active properties until he eventually sold it to Twentieth Century Fox.

*   *   *

I spent many nights running movies at the studio, trying to catch up with what other people were doing on film. I went to previews held by other studios. I began to better understand the kind of material that was being made and—obviously—the kind that was the most frequently bought.

I continued to be curious about how the studios bought their stories. There were no exclusively "literary" agents at that time. Every major talent agency had one person, sometimes only a secretary, to look after writer clients. Many directors worked from their own ideas, which they enlarged into a shooting script. These directors were so important that they would not let anyone act for them but the actual head of the agency.

It was a somewhat intimidating system, but I had no intention of being shouted down or cowed by anybody. I decided to act like a magazine editor.

I bombarded David with suggestions day and night. This resulted in his putting almost a dozen of my ideas on the advance RKO schedule; he thought it was worth the time and money required to develop them.

"Take one of these, put a writer on it, and see what you come up with!" he said. Suddenly I was a producer. I did not know it then, but I was about to produce thirteen films, discover a famous actress, and end up being courted by some of the biggest movie men in town. But at the beginning, I wasn't even sure of where to begin.

So I started with what I knew best: searching for a writer. I found Ben Markson through the pictures he had scripted while with Warner Brothers. I told David that we should make a film based on the life of Harry Reichenbach, the last of the great high-powered press agents. The Reichenbach story would give us the opportunity to portray some of the bizarre stunts that he had pulled off in an effort to promote his products. For example, to hype TARZAN, Reichenbach had checked into a New York hotel with a pet tiger. He then ordered lunch from the kitchen—a lunch consisting of cottage cheese and salad for himself and twenty-five pounds of hamburger meat for the cat.

Well, Ben and I wrote the Reichenbach story and script in the time it takes to sneeze. The resulting film, entitled THE HALF-NAKED TRUTH, was a successful, modest-budget show starring Lee

Tracy. I really didn't want it, but I was given a writer's screen credit. I had not come to California to be a screenwriter. I wanted a chance to produce.

Selznick quickly loaded me with projects—some of which he knew would not fly. No fuss. He would throw four or five projects at me within a week. I think he was trying to kill me and thereby put an end to my needling him. Whenever we had a disagreement over a story, he laughed it off, saying, "Well, you were right about *State Fair*. Maybe this is another one like it."

I had a friend, Nunally Johnson, who was at that time working at Paramount. He said that he would move to RKO if I could get him a proper contract; that way, we could work together. I strongly urged David to sign him, but while David was "thinking about it," Nunally's comedy, MOMMA LOVES POPPA, starring Charles Ruggles, came out to rave reviews. They called it the "sleeper of the year." With this great success, Paramount locked him in with a new contract, and he was lost to us. He later went on to become one of Hollywood's top writer/producers, with such classics as THE GRAPES OF WRATH.

*   *   *

Very quietly I went over the list of properties owned by the studio and saw nothing that seemed exciting. I decided to contact Maureen Watkins, who had written a play, *Chicago*, that was very successful. We kicked around some ideas on the telephone, but nothing ignited her. Two weeks later, she sent me the first act of a spoof on the broadcasting business, focusing on how a sponsor sells a product endorsement to a player and then to the public. We made a quick deal, and Maureen came to Hollywood, where she did the screenplay for a film called PROFESSIONAL SWEETHEART.

I cast an unknown girl, Ginger Rogers, in the leading part. Mervyn Le Roy had used this pretty and multi-talented actress in GOLDDIGGERS OF 1933, a film that he directed. When I saw her screen test, I gave her the role at once. The budget was very low, and the picture came in ahead of schedule. The reviews were laudatory, and a long and successful career was launched for the star.

Then Selznick got the idea that RKO should have a weekly radio program, the main purpose of which would be to promote our movies. He told me to "organize and get it started." Each week we put a star on the air to tell the story of the movie he or she had just made. Often we included the photographer and sound men to explain some of what happens during the shooting of a picture. Once a location manager described how a stunt was set up under different conditions. Another time a writer told why a certain locale had caught his interest.

We tried to tell our listeners of the colorful and interesting things that went into the making of a movie. After a few weeks, I got a New York call from Deac Aylesworth, head of NBC, saying that he liked what he had heard and asking me to come to New York to see him. His idea was to expand the program, and he felt that it could be a real success if it included all the studios, not just RKO.

I talked with my friend Howard Strickling, publicity manager at MGM, who predicted that L.B. Mayer would not cooperate, because he would want the show to be all about Metro pictures. Selznick listened to what Aylesworth wanted and said that this would be a big operation, one that he had never planned, and that he felt it would take too much of his time and attention. Instead of plugging every studio's projects on the air, we should be filling the stages with new shows of our own. "Besides," he said, "I need you in the film end. Radio is a whole new ball game for us." He lost interest in the program overnight.

*   *   *

My early experience with directors was very interesting. I found that some of them, like J. Walter Rubin, were almost impossible to cooperate with, and others, like William Seiter, followed the script that was handed them and you never had to worry about surprises. One brilliant guy, Gregory La Cava, who directed MY MAN GODFREY, also directed THE AGE OF CONSENT—with the help of a daily tub of cold beer on the set. Although he was a golfing buddy and close friend of W.C. Fields, his liquid capacity was not up to the comedian's. Much to my surprise, however, the picture came out just fine, and I gained another credit.

I saw some short films that had been made for Hal Roach under the direction of George Stevens and

Mark Sandrich. I persuaded Selznick to give them their first feature jobs on two of my shows. Not only were they great, but they went on to even greater successes elsewhere. George directed the memorable ALICE ADAMS for us, and Mark did HIPS, HIPS, HOORAY!, the best of the Wheeler-Woolsey comedies, which I produced.

But it was not all easy sledding. One day Selznick called me into his office and said, "I want you to make the next feature with Constance Bennett." Connie was the only really big star that RKO had then, and her film, WHAT PRICE HOLLYWOOD, had been a big money-maker. I asked, "What's the story?" Selznick answered, "No story. Connie just has an idea for a picture."

I looked my boss straight in the eye. "No thanks, David," I said. "I have to start with a story that has a beginning, a middle, and an end. You have a big investment in her. It would be foolish to entrust this to me." He wouldn't let me off the picture though, no matter how hard I protested. "Don't forget," he told me, "we're paying her thirty thousand a week, every week. We have to start shooting *something!*"

Miss Bennett raised holy hell with anybody and everybody on the RKO lot. Nothing seemed to please her. She expected to have the approval of even the bit players. The only thing that she really liked was the thirty-thousand-dollar check each week. She found no fault with that.

Since Connie would not come to the studio for

a meeting with either me or the director, George Archinbaud, we went to her home. It turned out that she wanted a romantic storyline, one that would feature herself with her companion, Gilbert Roland. We floundered around for weeks. She had a new idea every time we met. Vainly the director tried to quit. Finally he started the filming, receiving every morning the pages of the scenes he was supposed to shoot on that day. The film was called AFTER TONIGHT, and it turned out to be a real disaster, as we all knew it would.

9

A Turn
in the Road

While life was crowded with work, there was still time for fun and games. I played a lot of golf in those days and joined the Bel Air Country Club, which boasted a fine championship course. I could never break an eleven handicap, but I did make three holes-in-one in my few years there. A large number of the club members were from the entertainment industry, giving me an opportunity to broaden my acquaintance with people connected with my field. My social calendar began to include trips to Palm Springs, Santa Barbara, and Mexico.

One wonderful New Year's holiday was spent at the Arrowhead Springs Hotel with Alfred Hitchcock and one of my future clients, Charles Bennett. Charles had written the original 39 STEPS for Hitch, as well as many other hits. We were snowbound for two days, and Hitch entertained us by describing future pictures that he intended to shoot, one of which was LIFEBOAT.

It was at this time that I began to get offers from the other studios. Several Paramount executives with whom I had become friendly wanted me to join their production team. There were frequent lunches at Lucey's Restaurant, across the street from Paramount. They offered me a long-term contract (my RKO deal was for only one year at a time), and I found myself considering the idea. I did nothing about it, however, because I had one picture shooting and another in the cutting room.

Then one day I had a call from Harry Cohn, head of Columbia Pictures. "I hear that Paramount has been talking to you. Listen, kiddo, if you decide to move, better come see me." I thanked him and said that I would be happy to meet with him. "Okay," he said. "Come in at three today."

I enjoyed Cohn. I had expected to find a monster because of the stories that I had heard, but what I found instead was a literate man, and a friendly one. "I've got Capra and Riskin," he told me. "We're lucky with comedies. The trouble is, so few people can write or direct them."

He talked for about half an hour, mostly on subjects unrelated to the film business. He knew a lot about automobiles and boats. I told him that as a kid, I had been a dirt-track driver at county fairs . . . in a stripped-down Ford with no brakes. We simply put the wheel in a skid around the barrel, I explained, making the turn with the tires spinning like mad. We could then tear off without losing speed. "Great stuff for a picture!" he said.

Cohn had a framed photograph of his yacht on his office wall. On an occasion when I took John Jacob Astor through the studio, Cohn asked Astor if he knew anything about boats. Astor replied with a question. "How long is this one?" he asked, pointing to the picture of Cohn's boat. When Cohn told him, Astor jolted him by telling him exactly how much fuel it took to run it. "My God!" exclaimed Cohn. "I never knew you were a sailor."

Finally, there were three studios that wanted me to make pictures for them: Paramount, Columbia, and RKO. When RKO at last asked me to sign another one-year contract, I had to fall back and regroup. RKO became a different place the moment that David Selznick walked off the lot. He had gone to MGM to form his own unit there. With every change of executives, our program changed; some features were dropped, some halted, and some added. New players, with new demands for properties to fit them, were put under contract. Indecision was the order of the day.

At last I realized that what I really wanted to do was to have my own business. I wanted to be a literary agent in Hollywood, and to be my own boss. When I firmed up my thoughts, I moved fast; the next morning I was on a plane for New York. In the Big Apple I met with several of the top literary agents to explore the possibility of representing their writers in Hollywood when I opened my own agency. Their response was overwhelming. The big New York agencies were so enthusiastic about the idea that they almost scared me. Their pattern, they explained, had been to try one West Coast agent after another, with results that were either uneven or downright bad.

Overnight I was in business. I spent some time in New York to evaluate prospective contacts in the East Coast agency business. Then I called RKO, asking to be let out of my contract with them, which still had a few months to run. After that, I spent ten days in meetings with agency heads: Harold Ober, Carl Brandt, George T. Bye, Blanche C. Gregory, and the Curtis Brown company. These were the core. Their backlog of properties was enormous. Their lists included many top playwrights and novelists, some of whom were on the current best-seller lists. Before returning to Hollywood, I was thoroughly briefed.

And so it was "Good-bye!" to the life of a Hollywood producer and "Hello!" to the literary agency business.

10

The New Kid on the Block

The year was 1934. Sunset Boulevard was still a half paved and half dirt road. Although rents were high on the stretch that ran through West Hollywood, I kept looking until I found what I wanted. It was a modest little building at 9018 Sunset, and I learned that the owner of the building had been waging an unsuccessful struggle to keep up his rental income in face of what the Depression was doing to everyone else. I negotiated a fair price, offered him six months' rent in advance, and he took it gratefully. My RKO secretary, Dorothy Duncan, offered to manage the office, and we hired a stenographer. Suddenly I was an agent, with an office on Sunset Boulevard.

Los Angeles was hot, and there were heavy rainstorms. Our office sprang leaks in sundry places, and we had to set pails and dishpans everywhere. Into this scene walked our first client, William Wister Haines. He was a former electric lineman, tall, slim, and with eyes that failed to conceal his fierce determination. His uncle was Owen Wister, considered by many to be the greatest Western novelist of all time. Bill had been sent to us by Harold Ober's office in New York because his novel, *Slim*, had been published to great reviews.

I read *Slim* that night. It was about the life of a lineman on a construction gang. The next day I took Bill out to the Warner Studios in Burbank. Warner bought the book and signed Bill to a six-month contract as a staff writer. He worked there for several years, until World War II broke out. He ended up as a colonel in the Air Force and later wrote a play called "Command Decision." We sold it to Broadway and subsequently sold the film rights to MGM.

Edwin Balmer, editor of *Redbook* magazine, offered me a year's contract to write a monthly page citing the best films of the month. The pay was fair and I agreed to it. All of the studio heads were willing to cooperate with the exception of Louis B. Mayer. He disliked competing with other studios and felt that I should check with him before writing anything. His reason for this, as he told me, was that "nobody makes pictures like Metro does." Since the other studio heads of course believed the same thing about their organization, I cheerfully ignored Mayer's views on the matter. With Louis B. Mayer, this was something you did at your own peril, and it was many months before I was again welcome on the Culver City lot.

I visited all of the studios, where I met with producers and directors, most of whom were unknown to me. Motion-picture producers for years had threatened to do business without the use of agents. In other words, they would give you a good old-fashioned boycott if, in their eyes, you had crossed them. That sort of "disciplinary action" has almost disappeared these days now that agents have more power than studio heads—and usually make more money.

Back then, the power of the studio heads was zealously guarded. My agency was barred by Darryl Zanuck because I had sold Metro an original story— "To Please a Lady," by Barry Lyndon and Marjorie Drecker—after Zanuck had decided that *he* wanted it. Zanuck never made an offer, but Metro did, for fifty thousand dollars. News of this infuriated Zanuck, who said that he *might* have offered much more . . . so stay the hell off the Twentieth lot!

"To Please a Lady" was a car-racing story that I described to my friend, Clark Gable, one Saturday afternoon while we were playing golf. "That's for me!" Gable said. I told him that Darryl Zanuck also wanted to buy it. "Please don't sell it to Gopher Face," Gable said. "I wouldn't work for him." After Metro became the happy owner, Gable made a fine picture out of it in 1950.

My exile from Twentieth Century lasted for a little over a month. I was readmitted through the efforts of Harry Brand, head of publicity at Fox and a great human being. He thought that my banishment was "disgraceful" and called Joseph Schenck to ask him to straighten out the situation. Schenck told Zanuck about this and then met with me, saying, "I don't ask you to give us first look at material, or preferential treatment of any kind, but to simply let us see a story at the time you offer it to others." We shook hands and that was all there was to it. A few months later, I had a total of thirteen writers working on the Fox lot.

Jason Joy, business-affairs head at Fox, negotiated contracts with us. Once he told me, "Swanie, you're going to be the biggest flop this town has ever seen, or you will be the biggest and the best agent." Known as tough but fair, I was not above losing my patience. Once when a publishing executive was negotiating a deal with me and managed to ignite my anger, I snapped, "Don't squeeze the fish. It makes the eyes bulge. If you don't like the fish, throw it back on the wagon."

*　　*　　*

Edwin Knopf, who bought stories and writers at Metro, resented the amount of business we did on the lot. He once informed me, "I just discovered that one third of the material we acquired last year was from you or the New York agents you represent. That's not a healthy situation for us to be in."

Because of this, Knopf made a special trip to New York to visit every agency that used us as its Hollywood correspondent. He told them it would be much simpler and faster if they sent material directly to him and negotiated directly with him instead of with us. Well, those New York folks were smarter than Knopf. They thanked him for his thoughtfulness and promptly ignored his advice.

*　　*　　*

When I met with Louis B. Mayer, who ran MGM with an iron hand, he took the point of view that I was young and had not been an agent long enough to realize the power of his studio and, incidentally, of Louis B. Mayer himself. I promised to take his advice to heart . . . and immediately turned around and did something that severely angered the autocrat: I submitted a property to one of his producers. One of our writers, Richard Sherman, had written a tender, romantic novel, *To Mary With Love*, which I felt that MGM producer Irving Thalberg should read.

I had great respect for Thalberg, a white-faced, thin young man who crouched behind a huge desk in an enormous office. I told him the bare bones of the story and managed to arouse his curiosity to the point that he promised to read it over the weekend. I heard similar promises from other people every day and forgot about it for the moment. But I had underestimated Thalberg.

On Monday morning, Mayer had me on the carpet. "You did a terrible thing to Irving Thalberg," he said. "He's not a well man, and he had to sit up all night reading your book, *To Mary With Love*, when he really should have been in bed." Then Mayer started to cry. I had heard that he was able to do this at will, and he certainly outdid himself on this occasion. "But no one ever told me anything like this when I was negotiating elsewhere," I replied. "You're right," he said. "Just don't let it happen again." And the lecture was over.

CHAPTER

11

The Studios

That same tender, romantic love story, *To Mary With Love*, got me barred by Sam Goldwyn. After I had closed a deal on the property with Darryl Zanuck, I had a call from my friend, Merrett Hulburda, who was Goldwyn's assistant.

"We're ready to buy the Richard Sherman story," he said.

"I just sold it," I told him.

There was a long silence, and then Merrett said, "Mr. Goldwyn wants to talk to you."

There followed a heated twenty-minute monologue by Goldwyn, assuring me that he would pay a higher price than the one I had just accepted from Zanuck. He also explained carefully to me why it was that he, Goldwyn, was the only one in town who knew how to make this particular kind of picture properly. He ended by saying, "My voice is gone. Merrett will close the deal with you."

My friend Merrett knew that I could not and would not cancel the deal with Zanuck, so he said, "Swanie, the man says to stay off his lot. He never wants to see you again." The next weekend I played tennis with Merrett as usual. He said, "You brought the old fellow to a quick boil. The steam was coming out of the top of his head."

It didn't seem to matter. Three weeks later, Merrett called. "Goldwyn said last week that he hadn't seen you on the lot for some time, and I reminded him that he had barred you. He said I was to invite you to lunch today. Be there at twelve-thirty sharp, in his private dining room."

I knew that the old Hollywood slogan was still operating: "I'll never do business with him again—unless I need him." I wondered what he wanted.

The tiny alcove that accommodated eight people was part of a sound stage. Aside from Goldwyn and Merrett, I was the only other person present.

"It occurs to me that I should have brought along my taster," I said, attempting light irony, "in case you try to poison me."

My quip bombed. Goldwyn had no jokes or small talk to offer. The movie mogul was all business. He wanted me to act for him, for a ten-percent commission, in buying a property owned by Mary Pickford, who was co-owner of the studio with himself and Douglas Fairbanks.

Magazine cover. (1928)

Swannie and his mother.
(1905)

Charles Bennett with his literary
agent. H. N. Swanson in Swanson's
office. (1955) (photograph by Lou
Jacobs, Jr.)

Alfred Hitchcock and Charles Bennett. (1939)

Swanson on the prowl on the backlot. (1960) (photograph by Lou Jacobs, Jr.)

H. N. Swanson with Randolph Scott and Kenneth Gamet, his screenwriter, at the Bel Air Country Club. (1960) (photograph by Lou Jacobs, Jr.)

(Left to right) Pandro Berman, H. N. Swanson, Eddie Carter, Jesse Lasky. (1955)

(Foreground)
H. N. Swanson;
(third from right)
Eddie Carter. (1955)

H. N. Swanson in his
Beverly Hills office.
(1960)

H. N. Swanson and Robert Ardrey,
Metro's highest paid screenwriter.
(1950)

(Left to right) Eddie Carter, Norman Reilly Raine,
Robert Ardrey and H. N. Swanson. (1950)

Double Indemnity. Barbara Stanwyck, Fred MacMurray.
©1944 by Emka, Ltd. All rights reserved. (1941)

The Big Sleep. Humphrey Bogart, Lauren Bacall. (1946)

Elsa Lanchester, Charles Laughton, Ian Wolf. (From the film *Witness for the Prosecution*.) (1946)

Jessica Lang, Jack Nicholson, John Colicos. (From the remake of *The Postman Always Rings Twice*.) (1981)

The Great Gatsby. Robert Redford and Mia Farrow. (1974)

Stick. Dar Robinson, Burt Reynolds, José Perez. (1985)

"Hotel." *(Seated front center)* Anne Baxter and James Brolin. *(In Rear, left to right)* Shari Belafonte-Harper, Shea Farrell, Connie Selleca, Nathan Cook, Michael Spound, Heidi Bohay. (1980)

H. N. Swanson today.

The property was a story entitled *Secrets*. It seemed that Sam had tried on several occasions to negotiate with her, but every time they ended up in a cat fight, the net result of which was that they were no longer on speaking terms. Maybe each felt that he—or she—was really meant to be the sole owner of the lot where they were both based.

Even Sam Goldwyn's wife, Frances, reflected some of the irritation he carried around with him on the subject of Miss Pickford. She told me little stories about Pickford's frugality. It seems that Mary Pickford belonged to a women's club that met occasionally at her home, called "Pickfair." Frances said, "She always presented the bill for payment on wood burned in the fireplace that afternoon."

Well, I accepted the job. I called Pickford, who said that she would *never* sell the story in question to Sam Goldwyn! After two more calls, I decided to pull back and regroup. Not long after that, Mary came to my office to discuss the matter. She arrived highly upset. Her hair had not been done for a while, she had grown fat, and was slightly drunk. I could not blame my receptionist for having given the famous actress of an earlier day a little bit of a rough time. It certainly was not the Mary Pickford that everybody remembered. "I've never been so insulted in all my life," the star complained. "That woman out there didn't even know who I am."

After I had quieted her down some, she said, "I suppose Goldwyn put you up to this. I'll never speak to him again. I've thought about selling *Secrets*, and

I was willing to talk with you about it because you have a very good reputation." Surprisingly, she named a price. When I told Sam of it, he said, "Buy it!" It was a high price, but he was willing to pay it so everyone would be happy.

*　　*　　*

Goldwyn loved theatrical scenes. Once when his studio caught fire, he played it to the limit. He dashed around shouting orders to no one in particular and more or less having a good time at the disaster. I was part of a small crowd watching the largest stage catch fire. Goldwyn spotted me and shouted, "Everything is going! I'm ruined! There'll be nothing left!"

Unfortunately, however, the crazy suit Goldwyn was wearing at the time survived the fire. He was famous for wearing old and outmoded suits to work, reserving his best outfits for occasions when he and his wife went to a dinner party, or when they played cards with their cronies. I never went out with the Goldwyns socially, but both of them liked to talk to me. I enjoyed our chats too, even though I knew they were likely just trying to pump me for information such as which producers had acquired what properties.

Goldwyn, in his own way, was a health fanatic. He watched his diet carefully, and the chef he had in his dining area on the sound stage had been trained to serve him the proper foods with a flourish. Sam's only exercise was to walk part of the way home from work at the end of the day. He walked along behind his car until he got tired; then he would signal the chauffeur, who would stop and pick him up.

Sam played a kind of game you might be tempted to call "golf" with his close buddies. They had the habit of making astronomical bets on the first tee and then settling up before they played the next hole. It went like that all the way around the course. They didn't actually fight with each other, but they did yell and negotiate a lot as they worked their way from green to green.

Goldwyn loved writers, especially those with voluminous credits and large salaries. It was almost impossible to get him to read a story by a newcomer. He never followed the careers of those who wrote for the screen unless they were the equivalent of Sidney Howard or Paul Osborne. When it came right down to it, in negotiating to take on a writer, Goldwyn did not fool around, but closed the deal quickly. Sam really believed that if a good writer wrote a good script for him, he would end up making him a *great* writer. And it often worked out like that. He told me once, "You're not doing a great business because you're a great salesman, but because you have so many good writers working for you."

*   *   *

Irving Thalberg was a remote man, and very few people could honestly say that they were a friend of his. He would never negotiate business deals. Instead, he left negotiations to MGM's business-affairs department. In addition to his regular duties, he was given the most difficult and the riskiest assignments, such as finding vehicles for one of the Hollywood legends, the great Greta Garbo.

Thalberg was excellent with writers, showing enormous patience when stories did not fall easily into place. He was sympathetic and helpful. In his unit it was considered normal for a writer to be given at least six months on an assignment. Busy as he was, Thalberg always found time for exploratory reading.

C H A P T E R

12

A Few Clients

Jack Warner was a man with quite a short fuse. I always got along fine with him, listening to his terrible unfunny jokes as well as remaining poker-faced while he barked orders over the phone to his New York office. However, one day his legal department called me and said that I would no longer be welcome on the Burbank lot. It seems that one of our clients, Norman Reilly Raine, author of the "Tugboat Annie" stories and other hits, had been very vocal about how little money he was receiving under the terms of his contract. He was saying that he was going to leave Los Angeles, "say good-bye to the whole fucking business," and concentrate on writing for *The Saturday Evening Post*, which frequently ran his stories about the foul-mouthed female tugboat captain of New York harbor.

J.L. Warner decided that I had put Norman up to saying this, that Norman had no intention of leaving as he had threatened, and that he was using the whole ploy as a cover-up to accept another studio's offer of a better contract. I denied having had anything to do with "getting him unhappy," but I said that whatever he did with his life was his own decision. It was true, however, that the *Post* was really eager to have more material from him, much more.

But no one believed me. Finally Norman himself—redheaded, Scotch-Irish, no-nonsense fellow that he was—cornered Jack Warner on the lot one day. It was a case of put up or shut up, and when it came right down to it, Warner put up. He laughed a lot and said he guessed that everybody could use a little more money now and then. He told Norman to go ahead and tell Swanie to talk a new deal for him. He did, and I did.

*   *   *

One day I had a meeting with Darryl Zanuck in his large office. I wanted to sell him a new novel by W.R. Burnett that I had just sold to the Book-of-the-Month Club. Burnett was the author of the Western, *Yellow Sky*, an award-winning film from Zanuck's studio. Like most movie executives, Zanuck did not like to read but preferred that the stories be told to him. I was about halfway through my performance when I noticed that tell-tale vacant stare. I knew that I had lost him. I stopped talking as Zanuck began to pace up and down the office. He wanted to change the subject, he explained. "I'm going to London in a few days, and I've sent my polo ponies ahead, along with the feed and water they've been accustomed to."

"That's a really big deal," I told him.

He said, "Water is the most important thing for your animals, and whatever you do, you don't change that." I told him I wouldn't, and then I said, "It would be great if you would give my writers on your lot the same care and feeding that you give those ponies."

Zanuck took a dislike to Carl Brandt, head of Brandt & Brandt, one of the then top-flight New York literary agencies. He simply could not stand the way that Carl, in his somewhat Victorian manner, carried a handkerchief tucked in his sleeve. Zanuck's dislike for him erupted one day when he took Carl by the arm, escorted him to the entrance, and told him to never come back.

The Brandt office at that time was represented on the West Coast by Myron Selznick, who asked me to cover the studio for him because one of his important clients was working there. My conferences with Myron were always held in his small home in Beverly Hills. He was in a dressing gown most of the time and rarely went to his office. He loved to "squeeze the grape," and it was just par for the course that he have two or three drinks during a long meeting. You could never tell that he had been drinking; his speech and thinking were always clear.

Myron detested most of the studios because he felt that their system had killed his father, the film pioneer, Louis J. Selznick. Myron liked me, probably because he knew that his brother, David, trusted me.

Walt Disney was one of the finest studio heads I ever dealt with. He was knowledgeable far beyond his own business field, and his interests were wide-ranging. Somebody at his studio called his attention to a serial running in *Colliers* called "Old Yaller." The studio, which had done no business with us to speak of, soon became interested in the property. This was not necessarily a good omen. The Disney Studio was famous for the low prices it paid for its properties, and I strugged off their interest.

It must have been the right thing to do. One day Disney's secretary called me wondering if I would have lunch with Walt. Of course I would, and I knew what it was about. I also knew that I would be lunching in the main lunchroom on the Disney lot, where Walt ate with his employees every day. They called him "Walt," inquired about his health, and generally it was all very folksy.

After we had plowed through the cottage cheese and canned peaches, Walt got down to business. He said that he would like to make a picture out of "Old Yaller" and added, "I'm in good with little boys and dogs. I'd like to offer you twenty-five hundred." I explained that this novel had come to us through a New York agent who had big ideas about price. No deal. Sorry.

In the weeks following that lunch, the business-affairs director of the Disney studios raised the price to $5000 and then, finally, to $10,000. He also reminded me that they had never before offered that kind of money for a property. For a while it looked as if Disney would never get that charming story about the old yellow dog. However, at last I did manage to sell the property to Walt, but not until after I spent three months convincing him that I wouldn't drop the price from $50,000. After that, every time we met, he would kid me, saying that I was trying to bankrupt the studio. I recently sold the Disney company the cable rights to this property, just to make sure that the story was all theirs.

*   *   *

One day when I was going into the entrance to Columbia Pictures, I ran into Harry Cohn. "Hello, kid," he said, grabbing my lapels. "I see you're still alive despite having become an agent. Have they kicked you around much?"

"Like you said, I'm still here," I replied.

"Good!" he said. "You're probably better off than if you had gone to work for me." Harry was my friend all of his life, and he was also the only studio head I could always get on the phone immediately. He used to say, "What's new with you?" and, "Keep punching."

I brought many Eastern writers out to the Coast under writing contracts. Most of them were name writers, who looked upon a trip to California as a vacation; since many of them were short of cash, the experience was a lifesaver. The big talent agencies had little interest in servicing their clients and did not have enough foresight to carry their writers from a low salary to several thousand a week. These oversights on their part made it easier for me to operate.

13

. . . and Writers

Many people ask me about writers Raymond Chandler and James M. Cain. Both of these men left an indelible impression not only on modern letters, but on the motion-picture industry, which had and continues to have great success with their works.

Raymond Chandler was a resident of Los Angeles and an oil-company executive. He turned to writing when he lost his job on account of using alcohol too frequently. He wrote splendid short stories for the pulp magazines, and received next to nothing for them.

One day I had a call from Joseph Sistrom, a producer at Paramount Studios. He told me about a situation in which he thought I could be of help. Sistrom had signed a contract with Raymond Chandler after having read some of his stories in a detective magazine,

Black Mask. I had just sold James Cain's *Double Indemnity* to the studio. It was to be produced as a film, with Billy Wilder as director. Sistrom's idea was to have Raymond Chandler write the screenplay.

Sistrom said, "Chandler doesn't know a thing about screenplay writing, but it doesn't matter. He knows the kind of people Cain wrote about. He's eager to try his hand at the material and would take the two or three hundred a week the studio would probably offer him. Will you be his agent and get him a proper deal here?"

"I don't know how he writes," I said. "I'd have to be aware of what he does."

"No problem there," Sistrom replied. "I'll get you some of his *Black Mask* stories and you'll see what I've been talking about."

I read the Chandler stories and I was intrigued. I took Ray into Paramount's business office, turned down the $250 a week they offered him and came out the door with a ten-week contract at $750 a week. Ray did a top-rate job and got his first screenplay credit. But he was still unsure about being a studio writer, as we can see from his letter to me written in 1946:

> Dear Swanie ... I don't know. I don't know anything except that the standard method of working with writers is not for me. I think it works for 80% of the writers in Hollywood, that through it the studios somehow get pictures they would never get and ought never to get, if they relied on writers having any judgment of what is a picture. I don't think the

system works for those writers who, whatever their faults, cannot work effectively unless they somehow preserve the illusion that they are doing their own writing according to their own sense of what is right.

As far as any individual style is concerned, they are completely anonymous. That is not the kind of work I want to do in pictures. If that is the only kind of work —or something much inferior technically—that I am allowed to do, then I have nothing to contribute. For this reason I will not work for dominating people like Selznick or Goldwyn. If you deprive me of the right to do my own kind of writing, then there is nothing left.

Obviously, the studio system bothered Ray. He preferred to write under conditions that he could control. As time went on, we made a lot of money and his fame spread quickly. When his income increased and he was "fixed for life," he became more independent about his working conditions. While writing THE BLUE DAHLIA for producer John Houseman, he had a studio car standing by for his use at all times. But the studios forgave him and did their best to please him. The truth was that he really wanted only to stay at home and work on a novel.

Ray once wrote me a letter elaborating somewhat on his feelings about writers and his feelings toward me:

Dear Swanie . . . I'd guess maybe there are two kinds of writers: writers who write stories and writers who write writing. There are a hundred clever plot architects for every writer who can do a paragraph of prose with a touch of magic to it on whatever level, on whatever vein you happen to be interested in. Perhaps some of the better magazine editors know the difference, but I'm damned sure the critics don't .... You're a sweet guy, Swanie, one of the nicest I ever met. In fact, until I met you, I didn't think it was possible for an agent to be a nice guy.

Shortly after I received that letter, Ray said to me, "Swanie, I've decided to look around for a new agent. You've been wonderful for me, but once in a while I get to wondering if something better isn't waiting for me just around the corner. If I don't find it, at least I'll satisfy myself, and if you'd take me back, I would never complain again."

"Go ahead kid," I told him. "I'll always be waiting."

About six weeks later he called. "Will you take me back?" Of course I did. After that, he was happy with us. He told another client, "You know why I like the Swede? You can put out your hand in the dark and he'll always be there."

Drinking and illness crowded in on Chandler. He tried unsuccessfully to kill himself. I think he thought that this was sort of funny, but he didn't want to write about it. Right up to the time he died, Ray indulged in his favorite pastime: writing letters to friends and critics, and to the writers he most admired, which included Erle Stanley Gardner, Ian Fleming, and So-merset Maugham. He even wrote to people he had never met, such as the president of IBM. "Do you know him?" I asked. "Hell no, I just want to know what kind of a letter a man in that job would write."

Chandler was enormously curious about people and what motivated them. When talking with people, he did far more listening and observing than speaking, which is no difficult task since most people like nothing better than to talk of themselves.

Although Chandler was often compared to James M. Cain and was asked to write the screenplays for Cain's work, he did not appreciate the comparison. He once wrote that Cain was "a dirty little boy with a piece of chalk and a board fence and nobody looking." Cain, on the other hand, admired Chandler and said so frequently.

One day Cain came into my office to see me. I had read and admired his novels but had never met him. He was a tall, rough-looking fellow with bushy eyebrows and a kind of speech reminiscent of his newspaper days in New York. At one time he was the managing editor of *The New Yorker*, and he had also been the respected music critic at *The New York World*.

"I'm looking for advice and an agent," Cain said. It seemed that he was unhappy over the discovery that when he sold *The Postman Always Rings Twice* through one of the big agencies, he unknowingly sold not only the movie rights, but also the rights to dramatic productions, television, and other options. When "Postman" opened as a play on Broadway, Cain went around to the box office and asked, "How are we doing?" The man at the theater, when he realized that this was the author of the novel, told Cain that he would be getting no royalties because he had sold the dramatic rights to Metro.

"I need a keeper, I'm afraid," Cain told me. "Why don't you take care of me?" The arrangement we made lasted until the day he died. Actually, Jim's books became even more popular after his death. In 1982, we sold five of his novels to films and to publishers abroad. His vogue continues high until this day.

One time he told me of a lion farm in the San Fernando Valley that he planned to write about. He called the story "The Baby in the Ice Box," and it first appeared in *The American Mercury* in 1933. The William Morris office sold it to Paramount for one thousand dollars. The picture was made, after which Paramount sold the rights to Universal. Forty years later, when I had a buyer for the property—offering fifty thousand dollars and willing to go higher—Universal would not sell. "It's a Cain story," they said, "which will one day be worth a lot of money."

When Cain wasn't working in a studio or on his own material, he would get in his car and explore Southern California from one end to the other. He would sit at the counter in drive-in restaurants and listen to the conversation around him. Santa Barbara and San Diego were examined thoroughly. These locales made a deep impression on him, and many of his best stories are set in these places.

Music was close to his heart. In fact, he married an opera star, Florence MacBeth. He wrote *Serenade*, which will long remain a classic. Warner Brothers bought it for $35,000 and made a film starring Mario Lanza and Joan Fontaine.

For a brief time, Cain had been an insurance adjuster, a fact that can be detected in several of his stories such as *Double Indemnity*, where profit was the motive for murder. The film DOUBLE IN-DEMNITY was the talk of the town, and Chandler and Billy Wilder received an Academy Award nomination for the screenplay, and Barbara Stanwyck the nomination for Best Actress. In it, Fred MacMurray displayed his ability to play a role outside light comedy, which he had always considered his strong suit.

Many top producers have authorized me to buy back Cain's story *Mildred Pierce* from Warner Brothers. Warner owns the rights to this as well as to *Serenade*. The studio continually announces plans to remake the films, but it never seems to get started. Joan Crawford wrote me a letter every Christmas in lieu of a Christmas card, and the message was always the same: she reminded me that I had brought her back into the movie business with her role in *Mildred Pierce*.

Cain had fought unsuccessfully to keep this film from becoming another DOUBLE INDEMNITY; the studio had added the murder plot, which was not in the original book. The studio had missed the point: the story of a single, attractive young woman struggling to raise two children on her own. Cain wrote, "Why not tell that story, which at least has its own quality, rather than a murder story not very different from every 'B' picture that has been made in the last forty years?"

The Civil War was one of Cain's pet subjects. In later years, he spent an enormous amount of time in research and writing *Mignon*, which received mixed reviews and never sold to films. He once told me that this was the only book of his that was a failure.

Although Cain wrote about rough people for the most part, his friends and acquaintances were generally cultured people, who knew how to enjoy the finer things of life. When we went out to dinner together, Jim would invariably suggest one of the best restaurants in town—the sort of place his characters would never frequent.

*　　*　　*

Frank Buck was another client I enjoyed working for. I sold his book, *Bring 'Em Back Alive*, to RKO, which made a very successful film from it. Years later we sold it to television for a series, and after Frank's death, I sold his life story for television, a sale that brought his widow some extra money. It had a run of several months, although it was not very well produced and had little of the flair and color of the man.

Frank came back from Africa once with a boatload of monkeys for placement in various zoos. His experience with animals rested on the simple fact that he would capture them in their native habitat and bring them back to New York, where he would fill the orders he had taken from zoos and circuses around the country. Frank was a big bear of a man, and very genial; he would spend happy hour at the Manhattan watering holes two or three times a week. He drank bourbon as I have never seen it done before or since.

Frank told me many things that I still remember clearly. One was that the bite of a monkey's needle-sharp teeth could be very dangerous, sometimes fatal, whereas if a tiger chewed you up, your chances of surviving were pretty good. In Hollywood, he often staged thrill scenes for movie productions. I remember one in which a python and a black panther fought to the death.

*   *   *

Very often a writer has plenty of rich material right in his own backyard and it is not necessary for him to seek out faraway locales in plotting a good story. An excellent example of this is Mary O'Hara, who owned a horse ranch in Wyoming, where she wrote the tender and moving novel, *My Friend Flicka*. Mary's story was made and remade several times by Twentieth Century Fox, and today it is a classic. We have sold this book to all of the European publishers, and it still has a long life ahead in many languages.

*   *   *

We started representing Damon Runyon after his *Little Miss Marker* brought home to filmmakers the sudden realization that Damon was not just a newspaperman-turned-lucky with his stories about Broadway characters. All of the studios wanted to sign him to do original stories, but he continued working for himself, and his work sold as fast as he completed it.

Twentieth Century Fox offered us a writing contract for Runyon, which he finally accepted. Because he had cancer of the throat and could not talk, I would go out to the studio on Pico Boulevard, where he held court in a small office. He wanted to know what was going on around town, and I did my best to keep him informed. He would write his questions on a pad and I would answer them. Nothing he turned in satisfied himself or the studio, so nothing really came of his tenure in Hollywood.

*   *   *

These were the producers, directors, and writers who made the industry what it was. I was on friendly terms with many of the great ones and survived as an agent because I knew what they wanted and what they could do. Most of all, I tried to be alert to the story potential within each of my writers—that great story that needed just the right suggestion to bring it out.

My office met no planes and courted no celebrities. That's not what being an agent is all about. My primary job was to find the best writers who were around and to get the best price that could be obtained for their material. A good agent will know his writers and the kinds of material they write. He will know their likes and dislikes, and he will be able to project in advance how much a producer will offer for their works. A good agent will read what he's selling, and understand it. Then he will take a look at the industry to see if it has recently overdone this kind of story. He does not have to be a good writer himself to do all this, but certainly he must know the rudiments of good writing so as to separate the wheat from the chaff.

Then, of course, there is the human dimension. A good agent has to understand his writers for the people they are, and know how their human traits affect the kind of work they do. Even the way they eat and drink (and how much of either) is something an agent wants to know about, and some of the writers who have been my best clients and friends have done a lot of both.

14

High Jinks

Through the years, alcohol and writers have had a close association. One thing, however, is true: no good writer can perform properly if he has been drinking. Some of the writers I have known seemed to do their best work when they were "drying out" after a drinking bout. Perhaps the urgency of lost time and uncompleted work spurred them on.

* * *

When I first met William Faulkner, he said, "I need an agent for films. I've worked on screenplays before, with fair success, but I think I'm difficult to sell."

Bill had written a script at Warner Brothers on the life of Charles de Gaulle. Nobody liked the script. It was Jack Warner's thought that a film on de Gaulle would aid the war effort by influencing the Soviets to sympathize with the United States. Bill had thought that the studio would put this and his script, "Battle Cry," into early production, but they were both sidetracked by White House disapproval of the subject. After many months of disappointments, he began to drink more than usual.

No agent likes to see one of his clients fail on an assignment. When that happens, it might mean the end of a studio writing career. Faulkner had worked on eighteen films at Warner Brothers but was given screen credit only for his collaboration efforts on ROAD TO GLORY, TO HAVE AND HAVE NOT, THE BIG SLEEP, and LAND OF THE PHARAOHS. Of all the assignments that were given him, the one novel that he had really enjoyed and had felt comfortable in trying to adapt was *Mildred Pierce*, by J.M. Cain.

Bill felt that his record in Hollywood was truly disastrous. When he asked Jack Warner for a release from his contract, he wrote him the following note:

> I feel that I have made a bust at moving-picture writing. I have just spent three years doing work (trying to do it) that was not my forte and that I was not equipped to do, and therefore I have misspent time that as a 47-year-old novelist, I could not afford to spend. And I don't dare misspend any more of it.

Faulkner was almost always broke. In Los Angeles, away from his plantation in Mississippi, he lived at the Hollywood Knickerbocker. After he picked himself up and dusted himself off properly, he became famous through his wonderful characters in a series of stories called "Yoknapatawpha County."

Even though his novels won extravagant praise, he never made *Who's Who*. Three of his novels that were filmed are *Sanctuary*, *Intruder in the Dust*, and *The Sound and the Fury*. Among the good films on which he received credit was THE LONG HOT SUMMER, starring Paul Newman, Joanne Woodward, and Orson Welles.

When his finances were running low, Bill would wire me, asking me to tell Howard Hawks that he was ready if Hawks was. This writer/director relationship was really a perfect one. TO HAVE AND HAVE NOT is a fine example of their joint effort. After its success, Hawks tried to keep Faulkner interested in doing another film with him. Bill always preferred working with Howard at Warner's, although other studios offered him choice assignments from time to time.

I once had occasion to ask Jack Warner why he had let such an important writer as Faulkner slip through his fingers. He only gave me a blank, faraway look, and I was not sure that he really knew what I was talking about. J.L. had never met Bill, and I doubt that if he had, it would have changed the situation any.

Writing is a lonely business, and I imagine that is the reason many writers start drinking. I've asked a number of them why they drank, and they've told me, "A bottle of booze is somebody to talk to, so you're not alone."

Faulkner was a heavy, silent drinker, but not when he was writing. He always seemed to have a twilight bloom about him. When he was working, usually at Warner Brothers, he would be as dry as a bone until one day he would unexpectedly tell his secretary, "I'm leaving for about a week. Don't go away. See you then." After that, he would put on his battered gray hat and say good-bye to his studio friends.

Eventually he would find his way back to the Knickerbocker Hotel, where he would be greeted by a male nurse he had hired to take care of him. They would exchange a few pleasantries and Bill would head for the kitchenette, where a row of bourbon bottles had been lined up, waiting.

The more Faulkner drank, the more clothes he took off. When he was naked, the nurse would put him to bed and cover him up, and Bill would sleep for several hours. During the night, he might get up and go out onto the balcony and shoot Yankees. One of his relatives had been a Confederate officer high in the ranks, and Bill was steeped in his history. He would act out scenes based on the general's memories of a siege. This could go on for hours until Bill had slain all the enemy in sight. "Bang! Bang!" he would shout into the night as he crouched low when an adversary had been sighted. Then he would return to bed.

In spite of his antics, Faulkner was a gentleman, with a genuine concern for his black employees, whom he had left to run his farm in Oxford, Mississippi. His favorite watering hole was the back room at Musso and Frank's Restaurant on Hollywood Boulevard. This was where writers met to console each other and consume decent amounts of "holy water." Among the regulars were Raymond Chandler, Lillian Hellman, F. Scott Fitzgerald, James M. Cain, Dashiell Hammett, Horace McCoy, and W.R. Burnett. Occasionally Carl Sandburg and John Steinbeck could be seen there.

When Bill would return to the Burbank lot a few days later just the same as when he left, all of the men in the Writers' Building would crowd into his office and visit with him for hours. They never suspected that he would win the Pulitzer Prize one day, but they did know that someone very special had come their way.

Faulkner's speech and thinking were always clear. While he was still "a young man in his forties," as he described himself, he had a love affair with Meta Carpenter Wilde, who later wrote a book about their relationship.

*   *   *

Of all the writers I represented over the years, F. Scott Fitzgerald is the one that most people want to hear about. "You represented Fitzgerald for a long time," they say. "What were his working habits? Was he drinking every day of his life?"

When Fitzgerald was working at Metro on a

screenplay, he would report early every morning and dictate until the afternoon. The only thing that he would drink was Coca Cola. He would place the empty bottles around the baseboard of his office, and when the lines met, he would decide to knock off for a few days and take a little refresher.

Drunk or sober, Scott kept a daily account of his expenses: items of wearing apparel, lunches in the commissary, and sundries for Zelda and Scottie. Even when he was devoting a few days to drinking, he entered in his expense journal "Socializing." He knew what a cashed paycheck bought, but at the end of the night, when his wallet was empty, he could not remember to whom he had given any of his money. So his journal simply carried the entry, "Socializing."

Scott was a picturesque drunk. He liked to do things that would cause people to talk. I am convinced that Zelda drank too much simply because she wanted to keep up with him. Scott had difficulty in finding the privacy needed to devote to his writing because fans and other writers sought him out and took up his time. Most of Scott's friends in Hollywood were people he had known back East, many of them drawn to the West Coast through deals at the studios.

All of the stars were fans of Scott. He saw quite a bit of Lois Moran, a friendship of which I doubt that Zelda approved. He was also friendly with Norma Shearer, who was married to Irving Thalberg, on whom Scott based the character of the producer in *The Last Tycoon*. Scott was enormously impressed with Thalberg and his whole mystique.

Many of the pranks attributed to the Fitzgeralds originated with Zelda. Once they went to a formal dinner party to which they were uninvited. They appeared at the door on all fours, barking like dogs until they were admitted. Zelda then went to the bathroom, took off all of her clothes, and proceeded to take a leisurely bath. After getting dressed again, she joined the party as if nothing had happened.

I remember one visit to the Fitzgeralds' big, rambling house on the Maryland shore. This was a popular place for their weekend friends, and very often it was crowded. Scott had a little silver cup about three inches high that he awarded annually for "clean and fast croquet." There were no dead fish allowed at these parties. Zelda usually wore no underwear. Free and easy. Those were the times.

Some of Scott's best stunts occurred when he was in the company of the rich and famous. I used to travel to California once a year, and for many years I ended up at the Ambassador Hotel with two of my best regular illustrators, James Montgomery Flagg and Arthur William Brown. We had a suite, and it was always a busy place. Almost every night we were invited to the home of one film star or another.

One evening we were invited to the home of Carmel Myers, and Fitzgerald came along. During the course of the evening, he was found to be missing. Our hostess discovered him in the kitchen. Scott had dumped all of the contents of the women's purses into a big kettle and brought the whole thing to a merry boil.

On another occasion, we were with Scott as we watched Joan Crawford win a Charleston dance contest at the Coconut Grove. "Let's get out of here," Scott said. We followed him to the lobby of the hotel, where he asked the night clerk to fill his hat with small change. Then we went outside, where Scott threw coins at the windows of the guests and hollered "May Day! May Day!" When we checked out to go home, he put his paid bill on a funeral pyre made by piling chairs up to the ceiling and setting fire to them. It made a happy blaze that the hotel employees rushed to put out.

Scott's obsession with money was well known. Once I went with him to say good-bye to friends leaving for Europe on a midnight sailing. Scott stood on the dock with a stack of crisp one-dollar bills in his hands, and as the passengers boarded, he would hand them money and a cheery "Courtesy of the French Line." He also loved to see greenbacks floating down to a busy street from a high building and watch the pedestrians scamper for them.

Scott had an ongoing curiosity about Hollywood previews, where the studios would sneak a showing of a soon-to-be-released feature. This was usually helpful in enabling studio executives to get a feel for the production. I promised Scott that I would take him to one of these previews, but I told him that he probably would find it uninteresting and certainly unlikely to give him the kind of inside look he wanted.

So one night I took Scott out to Glendale for a sneak preview of a Universal picture. He was unusually quiet after the showing, and when we drove back to Hollywood, he asked, "Could we go past the Universal Studio?"

Once there, he was interested in a company that was shooting under the big arc lights. This is really what he had come to see. When we left the lot, we were joined by Buddy de Sylva, who was there to check on some footage from a picture he was producing. Buddy at that time was a top independent producer at Paramount and had previously been the boss on the lot. I introduced de Sylva to Fitzgerald, who was pleased to meet the man whose popular songs he had enjoyed so much.

"Don't leave yet," Buddy said, grabbing Scott by the elbow. "I have a little unfinished business to attend to." He took us through the big door opening into the reception room, unzipped his trousers, and urinated. "Gentlemen," he said, "this is what I think of the pictures they've been making."

Walter Wanger once decided to make a picture called WINTER CARNIVAL, focusing on the whoop-de-doo that goes on every year at Dartmouth College. It is a festive occasion, with skiing, house parties, drinking, and what have you. Budd Schulberg, a Dartmouth alumnus, was signed to develop the story.

Wanger wanted to stress the romantic love angle, and I suggested that Scott Fitzgerald be brought in. Budd and Scott got along fine, so off they went to the bitter cold of New Hampshire. Almost immediately, Scott got the flu. Large amounts of liquor did not effect a cure. The result was that he could not work and the whole trip was canceled before anything was written. Scott returned to New York and went into a hospital, where he was saved from pneumonia.

* * *

In the early days, John O'Hara was an ugly drunk . . . by his own admission. I never actually saw this, but people told me that he often sat in the waiting room at Twenty-One, where he would deliberately stick his feet out, thereby frequently tripping arriving diners. His father, a doctor in the coal region of Pennsylvania, often told him, "John, cut out the booze or you'll die before thirty." Well he did stop drinking, but not until years later. When I asked him why he had stopped, he said, "I just made up my mind."

O'Hara, like a thoroughbred horse, had a special stall for his own. Sometimes he tried to kick the hell out of it just to show the groom he was boss. As a brash, talented reporter in New York, he had made his fame with *Appointment in Samarra*. Then he wrote several very successful stories about a larcenous heel whose specialty was pursuing well-to-do women. Soon *Pal Joey* was a hit Broadway show.

At about this time, I got my hands on him . . . and found that my hands were full indeed. I finally stopped worrying when I realized that he was a pussycat to handle if you gave him what he wanted. His confidence in me was flattering. I showed O'Hara how he could make more money by writing original screen stories in the comfort of his home than by writing on assignment for the studios. Darryl Zanuck at Twentieth Century Fox paid $75,000 each for three originals.

John's ear for dialogue has been highly praised, and all of his works became big earners. MGM's BUTTERFIELD EIGHT is bringing in hefty royalties for his estate many years after its first release. Two of Zanuck's biggest successes were FROM THE TERRACE and TEN NORTH FREDERICK. A television series was based on his *Gibbsville* stories.

John told me that he had been able to give up drinking by just making up his mind to it, but it is very likely that a stay in Columbia Hospital, where he recovered from near death one night, helped him to do it. He had a gastric ulcer that hemorrhaged, and after that experience, he was placed on a strict diet, with no alcohol for the rest of his life.

O'Hara's friend, David Brown, once told me, "John is a real snob, you know. When he went to England, he took his Rolls with him. You'll never catch him upstairs at Twenty-One. The only reason he thinks you're good enough to represent him is that he remembers you as an editor, movie producer, and bank director. You're the only literary agent in *Who's Who in America*, and your real estate is worth more than his."

Well, anyway, John and I learned to live with one another. His way of beginning a phone call was by shouting at our switchboard operator, "Don't you know that when you call me, you must put Swanson on the line first so that I don't have to wait?" I'm afraid that, in his own way, O'Hara tolerated, or maybe even liked, me.

*　　*　　*

Charles Bennett and Alfred Hitchcock were quite a team, working and drinking together. One time they chartered a boat on the Thames and took along a band that played popular jazz songs as they went back and forth on the river.

We had many clients who preferred Scotch. Neil Patterson introduced me to Glenlivet Scotch. Neil was a champion golfer at Glen Eagles Country Club in Scotland; he arrived in Manhattan carrying a four-wood and little else. He could play twenty-seven holes of golf nonstop, then get charged up with Glenlivet. He had more trick shots than Ben Hogan and could use his four-wood from anywhere on the course, including sand traps. He wrote *Room at the Top*, which was not only a runaway favorite of both American and British critics, but was made into a film starring Laurence Harvey and Simone Signoret. It won Simone a well-deserved Academy Award and was voted best screenplay in England as well as America. After working at Metro for almost a year, Neil went back to Scotland to run a television company.

Some of our other clients were exclusive bour-

bon drinkers. When Fred Gipson arrived in Hollywood to work on the script of his novel, *Old Yaller*,
he too had little luggage for a stay of many months,
but he carried in a brown paper bag a quart of bourbon
whiskey. He said that he depended on it "like it was
mother's milk."

Among the two-fisted drinking clients I have
had, I would mention James M. Cain, Joseph Hayes,
and Victor Canning, whose sales records with us
were indeed flashy. W.R. Burnett was more an observer of than a participant in the Prohibition era in
Chicago, but he kept up with the others to say the
least.

Cain was a fellow with an enormous appetite
for life, and particularly for food and drink. I can see
him now, sitting with Alex Perino, owner of Perino's
Restaurant on Wilshire Boulevard, surrounded with
drinks. Perino, a polished, sophisticated chef, was
fascinated by the stories Cain told him about the
darker side of Manhattan. As Jim's dinners with Alex
became increasingly lengthy, his tales only further
intrigued the owner. To keep him talking, Alex made
him sample all of the after-dinner drinks the restaurant stocked. Jim would get drunk in a charming
way—that is, never falling-down drunk.

Two of our famous people, John O'Hara and
Elmore Leonard, had been heavy drinkers before join-
ing Alcoholics Anonymous. When John was pumped
up, he was not a very nice citizen, as I indicated
previously. Once I asked him, "How long has it been
since you've had a drink?" and he gave me the an-

swer by year, month, and number of days. Elmore Leonard, early on, drank quite a bit. Then, after he had joined A.A., he told me that he had his last drink at 9:00 A.M., January 24, 1977. Not a drop since.

One day I asked Raymond Chandler why he drank so much, and so steadily. "Simple," he replied. "Whenever a scene that you're trying to write isn't going so well, you can look at the bottle on your desk and realize that you have a friend there. It sort of loosens you up. The room isn't so lonely then." However, his "friend" betrayed him at the very time that success came suddenly and with a rush. He could not overcome a mental block on a book for which he was committed; he tried to commit suicide, but his revolver misfired. He died in La Jolla, California, on March 26, 1959, at the age of 71.

CHAPTER

15

A Problem
Is Solved

Drinking, of course, isn't the only way that people can put themselves through hell. Many of my clients were constant smokers, and I had a problem in that area myself. Consequently, I have a lot of empathy with chain smokers, especially when they are trying to break the habit. At one time I was a two-pack-a-day smoker, and if I stopped for a few days, somehow I found that I had to go back to smoking again. This is the story of how I quit.

At the time, I had a client, Harry Tugend, one of the highest-paid comedy writers in the business, with credits that would make your head spin. He was a top celebrity in town and the wit behind CAUGHT IN THE DRAFT, with Bob Hope, and A SOUTHERN YANKEE, with Red Skelton. He also created all the Frank Sinatra/Gene Kelly pictures, as well as many of the Ginger Rogers/Fred Astaire and Bob Hope/Bing Crosby films.

I negotiated with Paramount on Harry's behalf and got him into a position as head of production at a salary of $6500 a week. The studio once requested that he "write a picture using everyone on the lot." He did, and it was called STAR-SPANGLED RHYTHM, a terrific hit. Harry did not really care much for the executive hat he wore, but he was responsible for the studio assigning Billy Wilder to direct THE LOST WEEKEND, with Ray Milland.

Well, Harry called me one day to say that he was thinking of making a new kind of aviation picture and was wondering if I could get Frank Wead to write it. Wead was the first man to land an airplane on the deck of an aircraft carrier. He walked with two canes because of a fall in his home—not, as many assumed, from an injury in combat. One day after he had returned from Okinawa with his uniform covered with war medals, he was walking up the steps of the MGM administration building with his two canes. A little old white-haired lady exclaimed, "Oh, you dear boy, have they hurt you?" Then she threw her arms around him and began to cry. Alarmed, he shouted, "Get away from me, you old hag!"

Wead did, however, have a wide streak of warm feeling toward people. Once we talked about the men with whom he had flown in the war and I asked him if they were really as hard-boiled and ruthless as they seemed. Wead answered with, "Just the contrary.

Most of the guys were in love with the girl in the sky and they never got over it." He was a tough guy himself, and a good writer, and of course I wanted to get him the best deal that I possibly could. And this brings me to the point about smoking and how I came to stop. The first thing I had to do for Harry Tugend was to get Frank Wead for him.

Since Wead was under contract to MGM, I told Harry that I would try to make him available for a loan-out. When I asked Metro if they would have any objection to Wead's working on Paramount's Marathon lot, I was given a quick and emphatic "forget it!" Well, I didn't want to forget it, but I didn't realize then that my efforts to get Harry Tugend a writer and Frank Wead a deal would cause me to forget cigarettes forever.

What happened was that I went to see Benjamin Thau, Metro's top negotiator. I told Thau that if they expected to get Tugend to sign a new contract, they had better let Wead do the screenplay, because it was a good story and he was the right one to handle it. I emphasized the point by reminding Thau that I could get almost any studio to pay Frank more than Metro was currently paying him.

Thau admitted the truth of this and then said, "We have a long association with Harry that would be upset if he got a raise elsewhere, forcing us to meet that price when he returned to work at Metro."

I noticed that Thau was watching me closely all through the meeting. I was smoking furiously, and I knew that he noted my nervousness. This gave him the negotiating advantage. I walked out of his office with the deal I wanted, but I also knew that I would never again smoke while negotiating a deal. I was ashamed of myself for not having been in better control, and from that day on, I have never smoked.

Of course one of the all-time great smokers of the silver screen was Humphrey Bogart. He had a way of lighting a cigarette on camera that made him look like the toughest guy in the world. I was a friend of his, and an occasional drinking partner. Many of the films he starred in had been written by writers I represented.

One night Bogie and I went to the Mocambo, which was at that time the glitter spot on Sunset Strip. Bogie said that he would like to play a game to see how fast the human system would respond to a situation it found unbearable. What he did was this. As soon as we got inside, he walked up to a male patron and fixed him with a tough-guy stare. "I don't like that tie," he said, grabbing it and cutting it off with a big pair of scissors he had brought along for the purpose. Within half an hour he had clipped the ties of almost everyone there. Management heard about it and tried to stop him, but the tourists loved it and the game went on. Some of the more enthusiastic victims even asked him to sign the remnants.

Bogart had an unusual way of terminating an argument with his wife: he would grab a garden hose and wet her down thoroughly. On other occasions, he would be the sugar baby, played with broad strokes and promising her anything.

16

Gourmets All

You would be surprised at how something as simple as eating takes up so much of an agent's time. A lunch conference on a story is most productive when the agent can get a producer in a relaxed mood. Then he can give the moviemaker the highlights of the property he is selling and mention the names of the stars whom he feels would be just right for the roles. More deals are made over soup than in the studio.

Sometimes the author of the property is also included in the luncheon, to give additional support to the conversation. Some lunches run longer than two hours and may even continue back at the studio, where the agent might show the producer footage on a particular film that his client has done.

An agent also devotes much of his time to

lunches and dinners with his clients. Some authors are reluctant to talk about their work in progress. Because Fitzgerald felt that it was bad luck to do so, I never pressed him on what he was currently writing. Usually I prefer not to talk about it. Of course a literary agent is frequently interrogated over lunch by authors who want to know if a certain character in a plot would be likely to do a certain thing. Whatever you answer in the midst of a banquet rarely helps; in fact, it often impedes the writer's progress. I would much prefer to discuss these things in the office, and I have discovered that this is truest when a client brings in at least one third of a novel.

One of my clients with whom I most enjoy eating a meal is Elmore Leonard. Once we dined in one of the cities he loves to write about, New Orleans. "Dutch" was born there, and although he moved away at an early age, he often goes back to visit and knows the best restaurants in the city. He is a very special gourmet. Perhaps he remembers only too well the hard times he went through when he was just starting to sell his stories to the pulps.

The last time I was in New Orleans, I listened to Dutch tell of his progress on his book *Bandits*, which has that city as its setting. It took some time in the telling because it is a good book, and I think that he was into the story more than he was with some of his other novels. The outcome was that we had plenty of time to do lots of good eating.

On another occasion, I took him to Antoine's, which is probably the most famous eating establishment in the French Quarter. When we finished the meal, he said with some amusement, "Since you're paying the check, I can't object too seriously, but one of these days I want to take you to a place I know of that makes Antoine's look sick. They don't just put a dab of spinach on the oysters and call it 'Oysters Rockefeller.' They go about the operation as if it were for Louis the Fourteenth." Later, when Dutch took me to the place, I realized that this was a man who knew his food.

John O'Hara was another matter. He had some very strong ideas: one, he never carried any money on his person, and two, he was convinced that the yolk of an egg was about the best health food one could eat. Whenever he ordered fried eggs, he would, with great care, cut away the whites.

Every time I go to London, I invariably find myself confronted with a problem: if I invite guests to lunch, they order what for an American would be a full-course banquet, complete with a variety of wines. I don't try to change this, because to most Englishmen, lunch is the big meal of the day. So unless you're ready for a feast, don't go to London for lunch.

Janet Green and John McCormick called London's Hotel Savoy "the golden spot of civilized dining." Janet never ate unless she was really hungry, but when she was hungry, she was thorough. "No meal is complete for me without a generous portion of celery," she said. "It's a great sweep for the system, especially for writers, who sit down too much."

*   *   *

Chicago has long been noted for good steaks. It has always been a town for red meat and red liquor. I lived at the Ambassador Hotel most of the time when I was working in Chicago, and the Pump Room was a delightful place, notwithstanding the squad-car sirens blaring in the street outside. Chicago was a rough town in the 1920s, but the violent activity outside never lured me out of the Pump Room to see what was going on.

MacKinlay Kantor lived in Chicago, where his favorite place was Ireland's. His fancy was for enormous portions of the restaurant's famous oyster stew, made with cream, not milk. Although he was skinny, it never seemed to fatten him up.

*   *   *

There are also some great food aficionados on the Riviera. I made several trips to see Robert Standish, who had a house in the beautiful hills behind Cannes. At that time, Bob was just about the favorite author of *The Saturday Evening Post*. One time between salads, he outlined to me the story that later became *Elephant Walk*, a novel that I sold to Elizabeth Taylor.

Standish and his wife never liked to eat at home, so every night we would go to a different restaurant on the Blue Coast. Some of them were really little more than high-class grocery stores, with their fresh wares set forth in tempting displays before you as you strolled along the sidewalk. Bob had a fondness for shrimp mousse. It got so that customers would go into one of those eating places and tell the captain that they wanted to order exactly the same thing that Robert Standish had ordered on the previous evening. They knew they couldn't go wrong with that.

*   *   *

Arthur Hailey is not only the author of *Hotel*, but a man who usually approaches the dinner table with his mind already made up. This saves fumbling around with menus, and if he knows of a particular dish that has agreed with him or excited his taste buds in the past, that is what he orders. Also, a glass of wine is necessary, and his hobby is to identify the vintage he is served. For several years Arthur owned a vineyard in Napa. He never made much money with it, if any, but wine was always a pleasant subject that he could discuss with considerable authority.

Arthur, who was born in Canada, remains a very special person for me. Every one of his books has been a national best-seller, and we have sold all of them for films. His *Airport* became a television series, and his *Strong Medicine* was a mini-series. Aaron Spelling's "Hotel" completed its fifth year and was, of course, based on Arthur's novel. General Communications committed to more than half a million dollars for Hailey's novel and screenplay, *Overload*. Doubleday gave him a two-million-dollar advance for the novel he is currently writing. And his works have been translated in more than thirty countries.

The novelist and his wife, Sheila, live in Nassau on a little dab of land surrounded by water, with his boat tied up at the dock. Arthur is very particular about his shirts; he buys them by the dozen in London, and when they are in need of cleaning, he bundles them up and sends them to San Francisco because he does not trust the laundries in Nassau.

17

Tall
in the Saddle

Many people think that writers lead sedentary lives. In most cases this may be true, but there are some notable exceptions. Take, for instance, Fred Glidden, who got out of college in the middle of the Depression. As a newspaper reporter, he found job opportunities to be almost nonexistent and he went to Canada to become a fur-trapper. Having no money, he was forced to live off the land, in the very hostile climate of northern Alberta. He described the life as follows:

> All travel back in the bush is done by trails very much on the order, I suppose, of travel in the tropics. The insects, of course, are beyond description. Once off the trail in man's country and you're done for. On the trail the "bulldogs" or horseflies, flying ants, nits and

mosquitoes follow you around in a cloud, but except for the low drone of the bulldogs, the irritable whine of the mosquitoes and the hushed clump of your own feet, there is not a sound to be heard; yet all the time there is that pervading sense of something hidden and watching that puts me, who am not used to it, on a fine edge all the time.

In 1933, Fred Glidden was looking for ranch work in Wyoming. He had traveled the West, moving from state to state searching out ghost towns, listening to toothless old Indian chiefs tell about their past exploits, crossing rivers and deserts. Life in the bush and wandering in the West were becoming a part of him:

All the glamor of dog teams, hunting, snow and snowshoes, living with a rifle, etc., turns out to be hard, punishing work. But there is a joy and complete satisfaction in doing hard manual labor until you are so tired at night that you could drop; when every smoke tastes so good that you'd like to eat it; when every meal, no matter how bad it is, tastes better than the previous one; and when you get the sense of completely fitting into the scheme. All that supplants glamor and romance, but it's better. If you spent a year living that way, you'd never, never be content to go back to an apartment in a city and live through the thousand daily irritations of living by the clock, talking when you'd rather be silent, shaving when you'd like to look like a bum, taking exercise as a medicine (not as a pleasure), haggling over money

and all the rest of it. If you had the courage of your
convictions after such a year, you'd note mentally,
"The hell with it!" and come back here for good!

Fred wrote to his mother saying that what he
had seen had overwhelmed him. The whole golden
horizon seemed filled with brave frontier men and
women, with their stories to be written. He was
worried that he might not fully capture the essence
of the Old West, its sounds, colors, and excitement.
What impressed him the most was the realization
that this was a place and a time in America that
would never come again. He wanted all of it down
on paper as fast as he could describe it—the magic
of the starlit nights, the glow of the camp fires, and
"the soft sounds of horses moving in the dark."

In 1934, at Greeley, Colorado, while on his way
to a ranch where he thought he might find work,
Fred met Florence Elder, of Grand Junction, at a so-
rority dance. Romance blossomed, and soon afterward they were married and went to live in Santa
Fe, New Mexico, in a house they rented for ten dollars a month.

When Fred decided to try his hand at writing,
he first studied the pulp magazines filled with action
stories; then he wrote about his experiences as a fur-
trapper. His stories went to almost every magazine
he could find an address for . . . and promptly came
back. He realized that he needed a literary agent.

He also decided that he needed a pen name
and came up with "Luke Short." Short was in fact

a real person who lived from 1854 to 1893 and was a ". . . dapper little gambler, saloon-keeper, and gun-fighter in the environs of Dodge City, Kansas, well known for his fearless exploits and also for such hair-trigger cronies as Bat Masterson, Doc Holliday, and Wyatt Earp, among others."

In 1935, Fred sold his first story to Street and Smith, a large producer of pulp magazines, for $130. He smelled blood and tore into his new occupation at top speed. In his first year of writing for the pulps, he averaged a very considerable, for those days, $800 a month.

Soon Fred decided to write a full-length novel the way *he* wanted to write, and as far away from the pulp formula as he could get. I kept encouraging him to complete a novel, *Blood on the Moon*, which was finally sold to *The Saturday Evening Post* for serialization and which opened a booming market for him with that magazine. This novel was a best-seller, and RKO produced the film, starring Robert Mitchum and directed by Robert Wise. In the years that followed, every major studio and several independent producers bought at least one Luke Short novel.

Fred was a writer with steady work habits. He dictated to a secretary because he had serious eye problems for most of his life. In an average month, he was able to produce fifty thousand words in spite of this. A Luke Short novel or story is a standard in the publishing world. Fred wrote fifty-one novels, all of them highly profitable, with sales continuing through the years at a steady pace. By 1972, thirty-five million copies of his hard- and soft-cover books had been sold. Obviously, many more have sold since then. Not all of his books are historical Westerns. Some are modern; others have a political or mining background.

Glidden was a close observer of television, and he thought that some of the series of TV Westerns were so bad, so cliché-ridden, that they were self-destructive. He felt that the public could get along without those greedy cattle barons, the heavily mustachioed villains, and the dance-hall girls with sleepy eyes and hearts of gold. Nevertheless, he occasionally wrote for television.

Although every serial he wrote was filmed, he really wanted to do a continuing television program consisting of stories about ordinary people in a small pioneer town called "Primrose," set in a time when the railroad had gone through and Indian raids were half forgotten. He saw it, more or less, in the pattern and tradition of Thorton Wilder's "Our Town," and wanted to include a school, a livery stable, several saloons, and a tiny jail wherein the rowdies were put to calm down. Fred wanted to show love and warmth in this town, as well as excitement. He never went forward with the project because the networks discouraged him, claiming that Westerns were not prime merchandise at the moment.

Fred Glidden really was tall in the saddle. I was very proud to represent him as a literary agent and am happy to have known him as a true friend. When

I put together a volume of his stories that Arbor House calls *The Best of the West*, I wrote the introduction with much sadness that he was gone. His son, Daniel Glidden, is now writing under the name of Luke Short, Jr., and has published two books with Dell.

The Luke Short story, though, brings up another question very important to most of the writers with H.N. Swanson today. A number of people have asked me if I believe that television hasn't killed the market for the book projects I sell. On the contrary, TV is burning up new material so fast that we have to keep moving faster and faster just to stay in the same place.

18

Then . . . and Now

People often ask me if my business has changed very much since the days of the big studios and the movie moguls who ran them. Although many seem to think that the advent of television has changed everything, the truth is that the fundamentals of what I do have not changed at all. The essence of making a deal remains what it always has been. When a doctor operates today on a man for appendicitis, he follows essentially the same procedures he used twenty years ago. He may have better antibiotics, and better anesthetics, but he still has to know where to cut. In the same way, a deal is a deal. Television does not change the basics very much, and where it does, anyone familiar with the business would know what has to be done.

I remember, I sold Norman Reilly Raine's "Tug

Boat Annie" to Metro. But I wrote a provision in the contract stating that the author reserves all of the television rights. The studio lawyer called me and said, "We haven't done that before." I said, "Just write it in anyway," and he did. Well, that series became a big hit, and it was made into two separate television series thereafter. Through the years, the writer maintained almost complete control of his work.

Today, of course, subsidiary rights are sold off in bits and pieces for as much as the traffic will bear. Contracts, obviously, have become more complicated. I would not even consider making a deal these days without my lawyer or accountant by my side.

On the other hand, business today is a lot easier than it was in the '40s. In those days, there were only seven studios and seven buyers. I would estimate that there are now seventy buyers. Some days it seems as if everybody walking down Sunset Boulevard is an independent producer looking for a property. Consequently, selling a script is much easier than it was back then, but fewer features are being produced. So writers turn to other outlets for exposure, because exposure is the name of the game.

Television, far from killing the literary market, has expanded it a great deal. The opportunities to get work produced and aired are much greater than ever because of television's insatiable appetite for product. And the mini-series, or two-hour made-for-television film, is a respectable outlet for an author. If he writes plays, for example, he will soon learn that dinner theater is a big business. Dinner theater did not exist before. And all the little theaters scattered throughout the city are showcases for budding writers.

Unfortunately, however, it sometimes seems that everybody is writing something these days . . . and they shouldn't be. Once it's written, the author uses every means possible to interest the right people in the project of his dreams. I myself am approached at the oddest moments. I have belonged to my country club for many years and have spent many happy hours there. This did *not* include the occasion on which my caddy tried to sell me a script.

Even the "higher" professions are not immune to screenplay fever. On the way back from my father's funeral, the preacher said to me, "Before you leave town, I want you to take a look at this script. . . ."

As a literary agent, half of my work is analytical. I read. I listen. If a man rushes into my office and says, "I've got a great idea!" I tell him to go back and write it down. If he then comes back and says, "Read this," I do, and *then* discuss it with him. I try to encourage or discourage the writer appropriately. Writers need an enormous amount of encouragement. But an agent should never offer foolish praise, because that's potentially destructive. When the writer discovers that his work is lousy (if it is), he will be angry with the agent, and the agent will have wasted the writer's time.

However, a little more than verbal encouragement is sometimes necessary. I remember back when I was working as a producer at RKO, a big fellow by the name of Horace McCoy came to see me. He knew that I was a friend to new writers, and he had a burning desire to write The Great American Novel. He gave me some of his stories to read, and I liked them. I found one that I liked very much indeed, and I passed it on to Merian Cooper, who was just finishing KING KONG. Cooper liked it and thought that maybe we could use McCoy in the studio as a rewrite man on certain kinds of stories, principally melodramas.

When he called back to see me, Horace told me that he had spent quite some time as publicity manager for the golf star, Walter Hogan, and that got my attention, of course. Apparently the last tour had ended with McCoy in the category of "stone broke." Needless to say, he hoped that I could get him some kind of writing job at the studio, and as it happened, I already had. I bought the story of his that I liked for a modest sum . . . and also let him sleep in an office on the lot, which helped him out with his rent situation.

McCoy was a crack golfer, and we became quite friendly. I took him along to my club, where some of the members were a little bit afraid of him because he was known to be exceptionally hot-tempered. They respected his ability on the links, however, even if they never became very friendly with him.

When I left to start my own agency, Horace was one of the first to ask to be a client. He brought me a novel he had been working on: *They Shoot Horses, Don't They?* We sold it to the studios, and it was filmed in 1969. It starred Jane Fonda and Michael Sarrazin and was directed by Sydney Pollack. It won a Best Supporting Actor Award for Gig Young. After the sale of the book, instead of eating inexpensive commissary food as heretofore, Horace blossomed into a regular at Dave Chasen's restaurant, enjoying a special booth that was always reserved for him.

*   *   *

Sometimes more than encouragement, an author needs recognition for what he has already done. A writer named John Ball created the famous Tibbs character played by Sidney Poitier in a film called IN THE HEAT OF THE NIGHT. A few years ago, when John was coming across the country, he stopped over in a small town where IN THE HEAT OF THE NIGHT was showing. Proudly he went to the manager of the theater to assert that it was he who had written the book. The manager went out front with him to read the movie poster, and not finding John's name, called him a fake who was only trying to get a free admission.

Ball did not wait to reach California before discharging his New York agent; he called him on the phone and fired him then and there. When he arrived in Los Angeles, he joined H.N. Swanson, where, ever since, we have ensured that he receives full credit on the screen and in all advertising.

The Tibbs character is currently featured in the television series, "In the Heat of the Night," and

Ball's latest novel, *Homicide Story*, has been received with great enthusiasm.

*   *   *

Equally—or even more—important than encouragement and recognition, is the ability to match a writer with the right filmmaker. In a case that I remember well, the partnership turned into the kind of thing that you forever recall with pleasure. I am thinking of Charles Bennett, an English import whose record can only be described as "sterling silver." Bennett began his career as an actor. Years later, when he was known to the world as a foremost screenwriter, he was asked to appear in a series of advertisements as one of the "Men of Distinction" for Lord Calvert Canadian Whiskey.

When he turned his attention to playwriting, Bennett succeeded in having eight of his plays produced in London and New York, including "Blackmail" with Tallulah Bankhead. Acting as a producer, he also directed many of his own plays in London. It was when he teamed up with Alfred Hitchcock, however, that he really began to hit his stride. Charles joined Hitchcock to make the film version of "Blackmail," the first English and European full-length sound picture. It starred the Czech leading lady, Anny Ondra. Hitchcock had made it as a silent film but remade it with innovative dubbing techniques that were, literally, the talk of the movie industry of the day.

Charles Bennett was brought to Hollywood under contract to Universal Pictures, and his list includes over fifty writing credits such as BALA-LAIKA, THE YOUNG AT HEART, and REAP THE WILD WIND. The Bennett-Hitchcock alliance resulted in seven memorable films, including THE GIRL WAS YOUNG, THE THIRTY-NINE STEPS, FOREIGN CORRESPONDENT, SECRET AGENT, BLACKMAIL, SABOTAGE, and THE MAN WHO KNEW TOO MUCH. Hitch made the last one twice, once in England in 1934 and again in the United States, starring Jimmy Stewart. Bennett later became a film director and directed more than forty shows for television.

I have had the good fortune of working with some of the greatest authors of this century. Among them are Mary Roberts Rhinehart, Sherwood Anderson, George Wells, P.G. Wodehouse, Ernest Haycox, Robert Ardrey, Alan LeMay, Peter B. Kyne, Walter Edmonds, Katherine Brush, W.R. Burnett, Pearl Buck, E. Philips Oppenheim, S.J. Perelman, Richard Sherman, Edgar Wallace, Lawrence Stallings, S.S. VanDine, Thornton Wilder, Philip Wylie, Sally Benson, Clarence Budington Kelland, Paul Gallico, Frank Wead, Max Brand, and Theodore Dreiser. Some of these authors are now gone, but I will long remember them.

19

A Few Eccentrics

Over the years I have represented a diversity of writers, with every type of personality and life history, and the reason for this is that I make my decision about a writer only on the basis of the kind of story he or she produces. I don't want to know if the writer's uncle is running Twentieth Century Fox or if his brother is Clark Gable; all I want to know is how well he writes; if he can write to satisfy me, I can put up with a lot of personal quirks.

Sally Benson, for example, was a real fireball. Her conversation was laced with anecdotes about the New York theatrical set, and with plenty of profanity too. She was eclectic. She would give you insider information on *The New Yorker* magazine and a few minutes later she would detail a conversation she had enjoyed with some little old ladies with purple hair. At one time she was represented by Alan Miller, who told me, "Never get into an argument with Sally, because she'll kill you." Actually, she once threw an inkwell at Alan and ruined his new suit. Since she was making a big salary at the time, he forgave her.

It was an odd situation when I sold the Disney organization on the idea of putting this sophisticated lady under contract. She was not Disney's usual sort of author. Here was the girl who had done JUNIOR MISS, and MEET ME IN ST. LOUIS, and many other similar hits. However, she was with Disney for a while and labored bravely to instill her special kind of madness into the Disney mainstream.

*   *   *

It is not always possible to predict from a writer's life history what kind of author he will turn out to be. Joseph Hayes was a seminarian, studying in a Benedictine abbey for the priesthood, until one night he escaped over the wall with a burning desire to discover the real world. And discover he did, editing plays for Samuel French and then developing a career as a free-lance writer. Joseph produced four major novels: *The Desperate Hours*, *Bon Voyage*, *The Third Day*, and *The Long Dark Night*. The author of several fine suspense stories as well, he enjoys sales to Hollywood every year.

Many authors are well known to the reading public before their works are shown on the big screen. Daphne Du Maurier was a client of ours who came to the serious attention of the American studios with her widely acclaimed novel, *Rebecca*. Alfred Hitchcock was brought to Hollywood to direct the picture, which starred Laurence Olivier and Joan Fontaine. REBECCA won an Oscar for Best Film and Best Photography.

Even the grand dame of British suspense fiction, Agatha Christie, has visited Hollywood. In all the years that I represented her, however, she came to America only one time, and when she did, she knew exactly what it was that she wanted to see. When she arrived in Hollywood, I asked her which studio she would like to visit.

"Warner Brothers," was her instant reply.

"Why?" I asked.

"Because they know how to make melodramas," she said.

So I took her to lunch in the Warner executive dining room, where she met J.L. Warner himself. Agatha was a rather large lady, and not over talkative, but on this occasion she said, "People who make films over here in America seem to be more determined than we are."

The long list of Miss Christie's works sold in America include *And Then There Were None, Three Blind Mice,* and the play, *Witness for the Prosecution*, which was produced on Broadway. The film that followed was beautifully directed by Billy Wilder and starred the following all-time great stars: Marlene Dietrich, Tyrone Power, Charles Laughton, and Elsa Lanchester.

*   *   *

People remember W.R. Burnett as the author of hard-hitting gangster novels such as *Nobody Lives Forever*, *Little Caesar*, *High Sierra*, and a string of other Bogart pictures. Burnett, like some of his characters, was not entirely unacquainted with the wild side of life. Not only did he have a free and easy attitude toward earning and spending, but he brought the flavor of a tough guy into his conversation. I think some of his disregard for coin came during the years that he lived in Chicago and roomed with a gentleman strongly suspected of being a gangster. This man would buy forty-dollar silk shirts and when they needed washing, he simply threw them away.

Few knew that Burnett bred racing whippets. One of his dogs, Dark Hazard, was national champion. Bill wrote a novel with that title and sold it to Warner Brothers, who produced the picture, starring Edward G. Robinson. The dogs were an expensive hobby, however. Even though he was pulling in money at an unbelievable rate, Burnett spent several hundred thousand dollars before he gave up the sport.

To recoup fast, Burnett wrote *The Asphalt Jungle* in ten days, for which Metro paid $75,000. He figured that if he could make that kind of money sitting at home by his bar, why should he go on a studio payroll? His production was fantastic.

*   *   *

Novelist Rupert Hughes was another friend of mine, and he said that he had mentioned me to his nephew, Howard Hughes, suggesting that we get together. Contacting Howard Hughes was a feat in itself, but when at last we got together, I learned that he was very anxious to find a story in which the heroine was involved in an action situation.

"I'd like to get a doll up in an airplane and see what happens," Hughes said.

I told him that at the moment I did not have a story like that available and suggested he talk with W.R. Burnett, who was having a run of luck on sales and who might give him an original story. Burnett agreed to a meeting with Hughes, but after a short time, he said that the situation was unbelievably silly. Whenever he had a meeting with Hughes, it would always take place around midnight in a darkened house with no servants about. Burnett explained that Howard was afraid that other producers would find out what he was working on and steal it.

After many meetings and after listening to Hughes propound ideas at length, Bill said he felt that any story Hughes would buy would have to prominently feature women's breasts. Hughes had shown him screen tests he had made of several girls; they were dressed in tight black satin. The cameraman had been instructed to put Vaseline on the fabric to enhance the curves of the breasts. It was hard to laugh at Hughes, because he made a star of Jane Russell with this and similar methods.

*   *   *

Cornell Woolrich never had to face such problems. He was under close watch by his mother until well after he was a grown man. He was a thin wafer of a fellow who always wore dark or black suits. He suffered from the apprehension that he might die any day. He was prepared for this calamity by having on his person at all times a small leather case containing medicines and vitamins of every description. He had a cure for everything except snakebite.

Woolrich wrote sparkling love stories about flappers, which was natural because F. Scott Fitzgerald was his idol. After CHILDREN OF THE RITZ was financed by First National Pictures, he started writing thrillers and his writing became less lighthearted.

He very quickly became a hot ticket, and every studio wanted to buy him. He lived with his mother in a hotel on upper Broadway. Somehow he escaped her surveillance one day long enough to get married, but the marriage lasted for only a few weeks. Woolrich was a lonely man who liked to visit dark nightclubs to drink and to watch the passing scene, but never to have fun. I was his first agent, and we still represent his estate.

*　　*　　*

Paul Gallico was a sports reporter on *The New York Daily News* when Harold Ober encouraged him to do short stories for *The Saturday Evening Post*. We sold *The Clock*, which was made into one of Judy Garland's best pictures. He was the kind of writer who would go a couple of rounds with a prize fighter "just to see how it felt." As author of *The Snow Goose*, he won all kinds of critical praise. I enjoyed playing golf with Paul, although I knew that he was unable to enjoy it very much because he had phlebitis and had to wear rubber stockings. I remember that his New York apartment was crowded with cats that would not let him alone, but would incessantly follow him around.

*   *   *

Frank D. Gilroy is a gambler at heart. He always has been. He wrote "The Only Game in Town," a play about a gambler in Las Vegas. The play opened in Boston, and because of unhappy notices, it closed quickly so that some of the main roles could be recast. Because of Gilroy's reputation, I put the play up for motion-picture sale on an auction basis, even though the play's opening had been disastrous.

George Stevens and I were good friends, and he often asked me about properties that might be available. Anything George liked, any studio would buy for him. When I told him about Frank's new play, he read it and said that he wanted to be at the first night's performance on Broadway when it reopened. The play opened and closed within two weeks.

However, George thought that Elizabeth Taylor would be right for it. He told Fox that he would direct it and that Frank Gilroy would write the screenplay. David Brown, intrigued by the material and sensing that it presented a strong subject for Frank Sinatra, bought it for $650,000.

Before production could begin, Elizabeth Taylor, who was in Paris at the time, was stricken with a back ailment and could not travel to Hollywood to shoot at the studio. Accordingly, the studio built a Las Vegas street in Paris, which ran the budget over twelve million dollars.

Sinatra could not make the picture because of other engagements, so Warren Beatty replaced him. The film was shot and Beatty turned out to be excellent. The Paris location required that a great deal of the action be set indoors, which slowed the pace, but because of the two stars, the picture enjoyed a fair success, one of many created when David Brown was at Fox.

David Brown and Richard Zanuck were an unbeatable team with box-office successes: THE SOUND OF MUSIC, PATTON, M*A*S*H., HELLO, DOLLY!, BUTCH CASSIDY AND THE SUNDANCE KID, and THE STING. They gave Steven Spielberg his first shot at features with THE SUGARLAND EXPRESS, and Spielberg went on to direct one of their greatest smash hits, JAWS. THE STING was a big Academy Award winner, and their recent efforts brought to the screen COCOON, and THE VERDICT, which received seven Oscar nominations. They now have separate companies, but their strong friendship continues.

*　　*　　*

Joyce Carol Oates is probably one of America's most prolific writers at the present time. She usually does at least two books a year and has won the American Book Award. Joyce, a professor at Princeton University, is the darling of critics everywhere. She recently completed *Soul/Mate* and is writing the screenplay adaptations for two of her recent novels: *You Must Remember This*, for Martin Scorcese and Columbia Pictures, and *American Appetites*, for Dick Berg at Paramount. Joyce's novels have a haunting quality to them that stays with you, and Hollywood is really taking notice.

*   *   *

Dorothy Uhnak, internationally known for her stories about policewomen, was herself a cop in New York City. She surveyed the scene with the sharp detail of a camera eye . . . as well as with tenderness. Her first sale, "Get Christy Love," was a successful TV series that attracted the attention of feature-film producers. We just sold VICTIMS, her latest bestseller, as well as FALSE WITNESS, for films.

Another writer who learned to observe and report on the dark side of human nature while walking a beat is Joseph Wambaugh. He was still a cop when he showed us his first novel, *The New Centurions*, which was a successful book, and the film, directed by Richard Fleisher, was good story-telling. His anthology, *The Headhunters*, was the basis for the highly successful television series, "Police Story."

*   *   *

I am one of the few who feel that Western stories are due for a comeback. Their demise was due to the rash of television series that kept grinding out the same stories without varying their act. One of my writers of Westerns was Ernest Haycox, who wrote *Stage to Lordsburg*, which I sold to John Ford. Ford made a memorable picture out of it called STAGE-

COACH. Since then, I have sold it twice to different producers. The story never seems to die. I kept on selling Westerns to Ford; Alan Le May's THE SEARCHERS was another instant hit that he directed.

CHAPTER

20

"Dutch"

Strangely enough, it was my friendship with another of the great directors that convinced me that I had been right when I picked a writer who is today one of America's finest creators of genre fiction.

Alfred Hitchcock and I had become friends when he asked me to represent him. I told him that I was really a writer's agent and had to concentrate only on authors. "All right then," he said. "Represent my secretary, Joan Harrison." I did and helped her to become a producer at Universal.

Hitch was an Elmore Leonard fan long before the public at large had begun to catch on to his unusual way with a story. Hitchcock persuaded Universal to buy Leonard's *Unknown Man #89* and was doing a screenplay on it himself when he died.

One day I was in Hitchcock's office when he took off his pacemaker and began to take it apart. It was a ghoulish experience, especially when he said that he didn't think he had much time left. "I wonder which day it will be when I die," Hitch said, musing aloud. "A work day, or maybe on a weekend." California was his home until his death, and Leonard was one of the last authors who intrigued him.

Elmore "Dutch" Leonard is a phenomenon of the publishing world. He started writing about men, mainly in the Western genre, for the pulp magazines. His father was a General Motors executive and wanted his son to get into a car dealership. Dutch hated cars, and so he restricted his expertise to their descriptions in his novels, in which you get a real feel for his characters by the cars they drive.

I found one of Dutch's early stories in one of the men's magazines and liked it. I called him up and asked him who his agent was.

"I don't have an agent," he said.

"Well, you do now!" I told him.

One of the first things I asked him to do was to forget about the Westerns and to concentrate on a different type of story. His writing was good, but there was one very important element missing in those rough-and-tough, all-male yarns.

"Put the girl in the story," I said, "and I'll make you rich!" He did and I did.

Almost immediately Dutch began to click with sales to Hollywood. Of his twenty-four novels, every one of them has sold to films! No other writer can boast of such a record.

Leonard's work has always appealed to male stars, and many box-office names have appeared in a Dutch Leonard film. Among them are Paul Newman, Clint Eastwood, Burt Lancaster, Charles Bronson, Burt Reynolds, Roy Scheider, and Glenn Ford. His political crime novel, BANDITS, will star Bruce Willis.

Leonard never works from a plot outline. He lets the characters dictate the action, which is a challenge to the reader. He is well known for his realistic dialogue, and one rule he has always followed is to never write about people until he has heard them talk. It has been said that Leonard has the best ear for the rhythms of contemporary American speech of anyone writing. When the *Detroit Free Press* asked Dutch to do a special feature on crime in that city, he got to know many members of the Detroit Police Department's detective squad on a first-name basis. Since he spent many hours in the squad room watching and listening, his descriptions of the gritty day-to-day aspects of a policeman's work are drawn directly from life. It was not for nothing that the *New York Times* called Dutch the "Dickens of Detroit."

Dutch lives in a comfortable, oversized house in Birmingham, Michigan, a suburb of Detroit. He has a smart, attractive wife, who is the first to read the pages he comes up with. Sometimes she gives her opinion by just remaining silent for a while, he reports. Every day he sits down promptly at nine A.M. and spends the following eight hours in the company of a legal-sized yellow pad on which he writes in longhand. "I look up at three in the afternoon," he says, "and say 'Good! I still have two hours!' " Dutch goes to the typewriter only when the material he is working on is really ready; he is a ruthless editor when it comes to polishing his work.

The progress of Elmore Leonard on the sales charts and the best-seller lists has given us great satisfaction, since it is coupled with critical praise. He has been published in sixteen languages and receives fan mail from all over the world. *Glitz* was on the *New York Times* best-seller list for seventeen weeks, and for this book he was awarded Best Thriller of the Year Award from *Les Presses de la Cité* in France.

Dutch's recent novels, *Bandits* and *Freaky Deaky*, were best-sellers in both hard- and soft-cover, and Literary Guild selections. Arbor House has published *Touch*, *Freaky Deaky*, and his latest thriller, *Killshot*. His sales continue to climb, and every one of his books has sold for film. American Express paid Dutch $50,000 just to use his photograph in their advertising.

21

Reflections

Now that you've met some of the very special people who have been part of my life, perhaps you will understand why I continue to turn down offers from the big studios. I tell them thanks for the offer, but it's not for this kid. I'm happy just where I am, where the new story by the unknown author ever beckons.

I am often asked how today's producers differ from those of old. A major difference is that today most people in the industry are busy laying track for themselves. They think they might be running a studio some day—and it may be so—but just the thought is enough to mix them up. Some of the younger studio presidents earned themselves a lot of hatred on their way up the ladder. They like to create a mystique about themselves, which, in the long run, is pure self-aggrandizement and does not help to make a film.

Some of the major independent producers who really get pictures made include Sydney Pollack, Jaffe-Lansing, Robert Chartoff, Irwin Winkler, Guber-Peters, Steven Spielberg, David Brown, Richard and Lili Zanuck, and Ray Stark.

In addition to these, the business needs more people like Jerry Wald. Jerry was a whole studio by himself, with just a bulletin board of ideas and a great creative mind. He was a story man. Jerry, along with Richard Macauley, had at least thirty big writing/producing credits at Warner. He had scripts and director friends and an entourage of creative people; he could make a film quickly and easily because of his tremendous enthusiasm and knowledge of story.

Jerry would get on the phone and say, "Joe, I hear you're looking for an Elizabeth Taylor picture. Well, I have it!" He would have the producer in his office that afternoon and the picture would be on the way. He would walk into Jack Warner's office and say, "I think we should do a picture of a chain gang in the South."

Warner would look at him and see the light in Jerry's eye. "All right," JL would say. "Put a writer on it." Then Jerry would suggest Paul Muni for the picture. This would really have Warner excited, and later he would phone Jerry and say nervously, "I don't think Paul Muni will do the picture."

"Don't worry," Jerry would assure him. Then Wald would go over to see Muni and start acting out the part. He would have Muni so excited that he would call up JL and say, "We've got to do this picture!"

Jerry and some other people like him were exciters. They knew how to excite creative people and make things happen. If Jerry couldn't find a writer for a project, he would write the script himself, and in a few days. Those men got pictures made because they loved what they were doing and had no trepidation. There were many of the same obstacles to filmmaking then as now. You had to get financing. You had to shave your budget. You had all of the problems of casting. But filmmaking was fun. Like kids with a Mecanno set, these guys could fix any problem.

Today it seems that so many projects are subject to endless committee meetings. The committee members keep rewriting the script . . . forgetting that the patient will die of improvements. The only way around that kind of fiasco is to entrust the project to a producer who has also been a working writer, a writer with credits who knows the ways of the industry. There are still a few today who belong to this school, and they are always in heavy demand.

I think that a major problem today is that many writers haven't lived enough. Producers don't ask, "What's the story?" They ask, "How old is he?"— and the younger, the better. Hollywood encourages young people to try to write for riches before they have had a chance to live and gain some wisdom and perspective.

Some writers ask me if I think that newspaper stories are a good source of material. They come in and say, "Hey, I just read a story about a woman who is suing her husband for rape." Sure, I say, this is a good story, but a hundred other writers have already read the same item. Think. You've got a mind of your own. Why chase the wagon down the street? Of course some of the best screenwriters are also newspaper reporters, but that's because they know something about life.

When James M. Cain ran out of ideas, he would hire out as a gardener or go to work for a small-loan company with a collection agency. Some of his best stories had their genesis from these experiences, including *Double Indemnity*. When a writer is at a loss for ideas, I think he should go out and immerse himself in another business. He doesn't have to stick around the mining camp; he can go out in the prairies, or any place new to him. He'll catch a story when he least expects it.

When writers ask me what I want in a story, I tell them that I look first for true-to-life characters. I enjoy talking to writers who ask this question, because somehow when I start to elaborate the answer, I can't seem to stop. I'll go on talking about a pretty girl driving a sleek red roadster, her long, blonde hair whipping in the wind. If at some point I sense that the writer understands me and is receptive to what I'm saying, a warm wave of pleasure washes over me and I know that he is mine.

What I want him to know is that I am in the

same business that he is, and that he needn't go any farther. That kind of close cooperation is really what being an agent is all about. An agent is a good friend, a sharp critic, and ever willing to offer encouragement when the writer needs help, which is only too often.

*   *   *

What does a literary agent do? Every sunny day does he reach for the phone and dial a lot of studio heads and bankable actors? Does he listen to tales of woe from performers in the picture business? In our business there are no rules, just controlled hysteria over black words on white paper.

We are only concerned with a few very good writers, the discovery of them and watching closely every way the industry affects them. If the writer wants to break into novel writing or T.V., we are there to help him.

Ben Kamsler, attorney, salesmen, stage play producer and head of our play department, is now in his twenty-fifth year with us. His trips to Europe are frequent because the literary and stage markets over there are demanding and changing fast. Ben has a sharp legal mind and is an expert on copyright. He knows how to reserve rights that are often ignored or "traditionally" given away. Well, many top producers and publishers will break with such traditions when the writer is good enough and the agent persistent.

Jerry Prenchio, a young college graduate looking for a job selling writers, almost didn't work for us—

"I don't know anything about writers, but I am willing to try." We gave him a James M. Cain novel to read, hoping he would like the author and would be able to get excited about representing him. After a couple of weeks interviewing producers in studios, he told me, "I discovered something you probably knew all the time! When I would mention a writer's screen credits, the producer would say 'How old is he?' Apparently that was the only thing that mattered to him." I told Prenchio to concentrate on the characters in the book and if he liked them a lot, a sale would be much easier to make. "Concentrate on them," I kept telling him. Jerry had a way with people and soon was clicking along in high fashion. His training here taught him all he needed to know about how to work this town and make it big. He had fire in his stomach and would never give up until he met success. If he couldn't get a meeting, he'd go up to the office and bang on the door. After he left us, he said he would never forget how the system worked for him. He made so many millions that I doubt he ever counted them.

Michael Siegel is the latest addition to our staff. Michael studied literature at Stanford and film at USC. He concentrates on new writers and co-agenting books. He recently auctioned a novel on behalf of a New York agent that went to Universal for a six-figure option. Next he signed as a client Reidar Jonsson, author of *My Life As a Dog*, and has him under contract at Warner Bros. Not too bad—for a kid.

*   *   *

In some ways, I have outlived a whole generation and in so doing, outlived many dear friends. But the magic of great writing is that it stays alive, continually drawing people back. What is nostalgia today may be a fad tomorrow. My advice to writers is, don't die. But if you do, don't give up hope.

I know that the style of agencies has changed since I started out on Sunset Boulevard in 1934. The vogue among the bigger agencies is for gleaming glass tops and modern paintings. But that's not for us. We're just folks, like your corner grocery-store proprietor. If we're out of crackers, we will get them for you.

To some, these recollections may just be dust for sparrows, but to me, those horsemen riding past were vibrant, special people. And, of course, every one of them was sprinkled with ruby dust.